The Grammar Tree

Revised

Basic English Grammar and Composition **5**

Indranath Guha

Kavita Guha

OXFORD
UNIVERSITY PRESS

OXFORD
UNIVERSITY PRESS

YMCA Library Building, Jai Singh Road, New Delhi 110001

Oxford University Press is a department of the University of Oxford.
It furthers the University's objective of excellence in research, scholarship,
and education by publishing worldwide in

Oxford New York
Auckland Cape Town Dar es Salaam Hong Kong Karachi
Kuala Lumpur Madrid Melbourne Mexico City Nairobi
New Delhi Shanghai Taipei Toronto

With offices in
Argentina Austria Brazil Chile Czech Republic France Greece
Guatemala Hungary Italy Japan   Poland Portugal Singapore
South Korea Switzerland Thailand Turkey Ukraine Vietnam

Oxford is a registered trade mark of Oxford University Press
in the UK and in certain other countries.

Published in India
by Oxford University Press

First published 2001
Revised Second edition 2006
Tenth impression 2010

ISBN-13: 978-0-19-567504-7
ISBN-10: 0-19-567504-5

Icon by Raja
Text illustrations by Prashant Nayak
Cover illustrations by Nitin Chawla

Typeset in Bembo
by Innovative Processors, Delhi
Printed in India by Print Shop Pvt. Ltd., Chennai 600096
and published by Oxford University Press
YMCA Library Building, Jai Singh Road, New Delhi 110001

Introduction

Many methods are now followed in teaching and learning a language. What strikes one is that no matter what the method, the importance of grammar in this learning process is accepted by all. Even the advocates of the communicative method, in which the stress is on oral competence, make it clear that a knowledge of the fundamental rules of grammar is essential.

But when we ask the important questions *what is grammar* and *how should it be taught,* we get conflicting answers for the simple reason that different grammarians and linguists have different theories regarding the nature of grammar. We thus have *traditional* grammar, *generative* or *transformational* grammar, and *systemic* or *functional* grammar. One must choose amongst these and justify the choice.

New theories and new methods should be tested for a sufficiently long period before being recommended. Secondly, we must remember that most of these theories have been formulated and the methods tried in conditions which are different from those commonly found in India. What should make us even more cautious is that in many important areas of language-learning, we now find experts recommending a return to a discarded older method, e.g. the translation-method in learning words (vocabulary) of a foreign language.

The Grammar Tree, a series of textbooks on English grammar for primary classes, is based on the 'traditional' view, the usefulness of which is being felt all over again. Effective communication requires a knowledge and understanding of the dos and don'ts of grammar. To achieve this end, this graded series introduces the basic categories and teaches the rules, taking the help of extensive drills and, as far as possible, the descriptive method and current usage.

Each unit explains a grammatical item or gives further information on a previous item, followed by a number of exercises to help the learners understand and remember what they have read. **Spell Well** (Books 1 to 3) helps in building vocabulary and learning spelling; **comprehension** and **composition** encourage the learners to exercise their writing skills and put their knowledge of grammar to actual use. The **test papers** monitor progress.

The Grammar Tree has tried to strike a balance between (i) the purely workbook type and (ii) the conventional type of textbook. Then again, most current conventional series offer only bare explanations and limited exercises to be able to deal with a large number of grammatical topics in a single book. While **The Grammar Tree** does not intend to impress by its range, it does offer a comprehensive coverage of grammatical items with extensive explanations and exercises. The aim is to help learners find their way slowly but steadily, to consolidate, to instill confidence, to teach learners to walk before encouraging them to run.

Suggestions for improvement and correction of any error, for which we must be held solely responsible, will be gratefully received and acknowledged.

Kavita Guha
Indranath Guha

Introduction to the Second Revised Edition

The Grammar Tree series has been thoroughly revised, reorganized and, in places, rewritten, not only in the light of our own classroom experience, but also in accordance with suggestions received from teachers of various schools and other users. We are deeply grateful to all those, specially Mrs Ratna Bose, Mrs Susan Jachuck and Mr Debjit Bose, all of Garden High School, Kolkata, who have helped us in our efforts to make this series as useful to young learners as possible.

Kavita Guha
Indranath Guha

Contents

Chapter	Page
1. Prefixes and Suffixes	7
2. Reflexive Pronouns	10
3. Possessive Adjectives and Possessive Pronouns	14
4. Some More Adverbs	20
5. Some More Adjectives	24
6. Contractions	27
7. Rikki-Tikki-Tavi	32
8. Lost and Found	34
Test 1	38
9. Verbs of Incomplete Predication	40
10. Sentences, Phrases and Clauses	45
11. Kinds of Phrases	48
12. Kinds of Sentences and Clauses	52
13. Prepositions	59

Chapter	Page
14. Active and Passive Voice	63
15. Direct and Indirect Speech–1	70
16. Direct and Indirect Speech–2	76
17. Dorothy and Her Friends	87
18. The Pobble Who Has No Toes	91
Test 2	94
19. Conjunctions	97
20. Participles and Gerunds	100
21. Faithful John	106
22. Whitewashing a Fence	110
23. Writing a Letter	114
24. Writing an Autobiography	119
25. Writing a Story and a Dialogue	123
26. Writing a Diary	127
27. E-Mail	130
Test 3	133

Prefixes and Suffixes

Prefixes

A **prefix** [Latin **pre** = before + **fix** = to attach] is a letter or group of letters added to the **beginning** of a word to form a new word, the meaning of which is almost always different from that of the original word.

In Book 3, you have learnt the use of some prefixes to form **opposites** or **antonyms** of certain words:

un– + kind = unkind   *in–* + direct = indirect

im– + possible = impossible   *dis–* + like = dislike

Three other prefixes which are often used to form antonyms are *il–*, *ir–* and *non–* :

il– + legal = illegal   *il–* + literate = illiterate

ir– + regular = irregular   *ir–* + responsible = irresponsible

non– + violent = non-violent   *non–* + stop = non-stop

Note: Usually the prefix and the word to which it is added are written together as one word: *dislike, illegal, irresponsible*. However, in some cases, a hyphen is used to separate the prefix from the word to which it is added: *non-cooperation, non-stop*.

A. Fill in the blanks with words formed by adding *prefixes* to the words given in brackets:

1. Though we played very well, we were .... and lost the match. *(lucky)*

2. Ram's answer to the question is .... *(correct)*

3. Jayant was asleep and was .... that the train had stopped. *(aware)*

4. The cooking oil was tested and found to be .... *(pure)*

5. If you do something ...., you will be punished. *(legal)*

6. That dress is made of silk, but is quite .... *(expensive)*

7. Due to illness, Sanjay's attendance has been extremely .... *(regular)*

8. He has brought .... to his family by his shameful conduct. *(honour)*

9. The man was too old and .... for such work. *(fit)*

10. John was .... and not allowed to run in the race. *(qualified)*

11. In 1920, Gandhiji started the .... movement against the British. *(cooperation)*

12. He was so badly injured that he was .... to move. *(able)*

13. No man is .... *(mortal)*

14. One must not be .... to a guest. *(courteous)*

15. In an examination, do not write .... things. *(relevant)*

Suffixes

A *suffix* is a letter or group of letters added to the **end** of a word to form a new word, the meaning of which is usually different from that of the original word.

We use suffixes for many purposes, some of which you have already learnt without perhaps being aware of it, for example:

(i) for forming plurals of nouns by adding **–s**, **–es**, **–en** to the singular forms;

(ii) for forming tenses of verbs by adding **–s**, **–es**, **–d**, **–ed**, **–t**, etc. to the base forms;

(iii) for forming adverbs by adding **–ly** to adjectives.

Let us now look at three commonly used suffixes:

(a) **–er** :   teach + **–er** = teacher   work + **–er** = worker

   (i) In the case of words ending in *e*, only **–r** needs to be added:

      sure + **–er** = surer   pure + **–er** = purer

   (ii) In the case of words ending in *y*, the *y* has to be dropped and **–ier** has to be added:

      dry + **–er** = drier   merry + **–er** = merrier

(b) **–ful** :   help + **–ful** = helpful   care + **–ful** = careful

(c) **–less** :   help + **–less** = helpless   care + **–less** = careless

B. Fill in the blanks with words formed by adding –er, –ful or –less to the words given in brackets:

1. The flood made many people .... and they had to live in the open air. *(home)*

2. The famous .... was asked to draw a portrait of the king. *(paint)*

3. The .... fell off the horse and broke his arm. *(ride)*

4. Barun had been running so hard that he was .... *(breath)*

5. Gautam looked very .... when he heard that his friends had come. *(cheer)*

6. Sanjay has made .... mistakes and lost many marks. *(care)*

7. A fly is a .... of many diseases. *(carry)*

8. The smoke from car engines is very .... *(harm)*

9. The child was so .... that it would not sit still even for a moment. *(rest)*

10. The .... you finish your work, the .... you can go home. *(soon, early)*

11. Mt Everest is .... than any other mountain in the world. *(high)*

12. The .... of a car must follow all the rules of the road. *(drive)*

13. There are many .... places in this world of ours. *(beauty)*

14. Only a .... of people turned up to watch the match, and the galleries were empty. *(hand)*

15. The dacoits hit the man so hard on the head that he fell down .... *(sense)*

Reflexive Pronouns

In Book 4 you have learnt that **pronouns** are words that are often used in place of nouns which have been already mentioned or are already known. You have also looked at one class of pronouns: **personal pronouns**.

We shall now look at another group of pronouns that are formed by adding *–self* or *–selves* to some of the different forms of the personal pronouns.

A table of these pronouns, known as *reflexive pronouns,* is given below:

Person	Gender and Number	Form of the Reflexive Pronoun
first	singular	*myself*
	plural	*ourselves*
second	singular	*yourself*
	plural	*yourselves*
third	masculine singular	*himself*
	feminine singular	*herself*
	common/neuter singular	*itself*
	all genders plural	*themselves*

Note that though in the case of the **second person personal pronoun**, the same form **you** is used to refer to one or more than one person, in the case of the **second person reflexive pronoun**, *yourself* is the **singular** form and *yourselves* the **plural** form.

Uses of Reflexive Pronouns

Reflexive pronouns are used when the *object*, direct or indirect, of a verb is the same person or thing as the *subject* of the verb.

(a) *I* blamed **myself** for the accident.

(b) *John* could not see **himself** in the mirror.

(c) *Rita* bought **herself** a new dress for Diwali.

In (a), the subject **I** did something – **blamed** – which affected or **reflected** back on the subject itself. As the object is the same person as the subject, the reflexive pronoun *myself* has been used.

Similarly in (b), the subject and the object refer to the same person. **John** was trying to see **John** in the mirror. So, the reflexive pronoun *himself* has been used.

In (c), *herself*, the indirect object of the verb *bought*, refers to the subject, **Rita**. In Book 4, we have said that the object, direct or indirect, of a verb must refer to a person or thing that is different from the subject. We now find that in some cases, the object and subject can be the same person or thing. This is, therefore, an exception to the rule mentioned in Book 4. To make this clear, when a verb takes a reflexive pronoun as its object, we say that the verb has been used **reflexively**, rather than saying that it is a **transitive** verb.

Reflexive pronouns are also used for **emphasis**:

(a) He cleaned the room **himself**.

(b) We **ourselves** saw a tiger fighting with an elephant.

In (a), the fact that *he*, and not somebody else, cleaned the room is emphasized.

In (b), the fact that we saw something with our *own* eyes is emphasized: it is not that we are merely reporting what somebody else saw.

Reflexive pronouns are also used to **emphasize** that somebody did something alone, or without any help or interference from anyone else. Note the use of the preposition **by**.

(a) Rita was sitting in the garden *by* **herself**.

(b) Rita cooked the fish *by* **herself**.

In (a), '*by* **herself**' means 'all alone'.

Sentence (b) makes it clear that Rita cooked the fish without any help from anybody.

When a reflexive pronoun is used for emphasis, it is also known as an *emphatic* or *emphasizing pronoun*.

Reflexive pronouns are used after verbs with prepositions to make it clear which person or thing we are talking about.

(a) Rinky is annoyed *with* **herself**.   (= Rinky)
(b) Rinky is annoyed *with* **her**.   (= somebody other than Rinky)
(c) Ram was talking *to* **him**.   (= somebody other than Ram)
(d) Ram was talking *to* **himself**.   (= Ram)

When it is clear which person we are talking about, a reflexive pronoun is *not* used:

(e) Ram can take this book *with* **him** to school.   (= with Ram)

Note that we do not use **himself** here, for it is clear that **him** cannot refer to anybody else but **Ram.**

Reflexive pronouns are not usually used in the case of actions that people normally do to themselves, like *washing*, *dressing*, etc.

We do not usually say: 'I washed and dressed <u>myself</u>.' We say, 'I washed and dressed.'

However, if it is an action that somebody is not normally expected to do, the reflexive may be used to express **surprise**:

(a) The <u>baby</u> fed **itself**.
    Normally, a baby is fed by somebody else. The use of the reflexive *itself* expresses surprise that the baby could feed itself without anybody's help.
(b) The <u>dog</u> **itself** opened the door!
    Opening a door is a difficult thing for a dog to do, but this dog did it!
    Obviously, the speaker was surprised.

Fill in the blanks with appropriate *reflexive pronouns*:

1. Shyam did not go to any school. He taught .... to read and write.

2. To find out what had happened, they all went to his house ....

3. I saw that exciting cricket match ....

4. All the children enjoyed .... at the zoo.

5. 'All of you must save .... by leaving this sinking ship at once,' said the Captain.

6. Rita bought a new dress for ....

7. We must look after .... and not depend on others.

8. Bina's mother told her, 'Go and look at .... in the mirror.'

9. The dog managed to open the door by ....

10. Jayant forced .... to swallow the bitter medicine.

11. 'You and Richard must clean the room ....,' said Ma.

12. The machine does all the work by ....

13. The child hid .... behind the sofa.

14. The animals saved .... from the fire by jumping into the river.

15. It is said that God helps those who help ....

16. 'You should be ashamed of .... for what you have done,' said the teacher to the children who had broken a window.

Possessive Adjectives and Possessive Pronouns

Possessive Adjectives

Look at the following sentences:

(a) I have lost **my** book.

(b) Where is **your** pen?

(c) She has forgotten to take **her** umbrella with her.

These words – *my, your, her* – are really *possessive* forms of the *personal pronouns* **I, you, she**, because they tell us about *possession*, that certain persons have or own certain things, or that certain things belong to certain persons:

My book belongs to *me*.

Your pen belongs to *you*.

Her umbrella belongs to *her*.

These words are, however, considered to be **adjectives**, because they *depend on* **nouns** (like *book, pen, umbrella*) and do the work of adjectives. They cannot be used on their own, that is independently, without nouns.

You cannot say:

(a) I have lost **my** ....

(b) Where is **your** ....

(c) She has forgotten to take **her** .... with her.

In each case, a **noun** – *book, pen, umbrella* – is needed to make the sense complete. They are, therefore, called *possessive adjectives* or *pronominal adjectives* (as they have been formed from *pronouns*).

Possessive Pronouns

Now, look at these sentences:

(a) John is reading a book. It is **mine**.

(b) My shirt is white. So is **yours**.

(c) That umbrella is new. It is **hers**.

(d) Is this house **theirs**?

These words — *mine, yours, hers, theirs* — are also *possessive* forms of the *personal pronouns* **I, you, she** and **they**, which tell us that certain persons have or own certain things, or that certain things belong to certain persons. But note that they *do not depend on* **nouns**. In each of the above sentences, the pronoun has been used without a noun, and the sense is complete:

(a) It is **mine**.   (= belongs to me)

(b) So is **yours**.   (= belongs to you)

(c) It is **hers**.   (= belongs to her)

(d) **theirs**   (= belongs to them)

These possessive forms are called *possessive pronouns*.

The table given below will help you to distinguish between possessive pronouns and possessive or pronominal adjectives. Study it carefully so that you do not confuse one with the other.

Possessive Pronouns	Pronominal/ Possessive Adjectives
mine	my
ours	our
thine	*thy*
yours	your
his	*his*
hers	her
theirs	their
	its

In Book 4, you have already been told that:

■ **Thy** and **thine** are rarely used now, and then, only in poetry and prayer.

■ **His** is used *both* as a possessive pronoun and a possessive/pronominal adjective:

   (h) This book is **his**.   (possessive pronoun)

   (i)   This is **his** book.   (possessive adjective)

■ The pronoun **it** has only one possessive form: its. Its is used only as a possessive adjective. We can say: The dog wagged **its** tail, but we cannot say: The dog wagged the tail of **its**.

Do not confuse *its* with *it's* – *it's* is really a shortened form of *it is*.

(See Chapter 6: Contractions)

> The simple rule that can almost always help you to distinguish a possessive pronoun from a possessive adjective is that a possessive adjective is always used with a noun and comes **before** the noun it qualifies. Since a possessive pronoun does not depend on a noun, if it is used in a sentence with a noun, it comes **after** the noun.

In the sentence, 'He is **my** friend', **my** is a possessive/pronominal adjective and comes *before* the noun *friend*.

In the sentence, 'He is a friend of **mine**', **mine** is a possessive pronoun and comes *after* the noun *friend*.

A. **State whether the underlined words are *possessive pronouns* or *possessive adjectives*:**

1. Rita says that this is <u>her</u> book, but I think it is <u>mine</u>.
2. Let us go to <u>her</u> room and see if she is in.
3. How can we give away something that is not <u>ours</u>?
4. Let me take <u>my</u> books. I do not want to borrow any of <u>his</u>.
5. Have you got <u>your</u> compass? If you don't have it, let me lend you <u>mine</u>.
6. Where is <u>their</u> car? They cannot walk all the way to that house of <u>theirs</u>.
7. We watched the tiger finish <u>its</u> meal.
8. If you cannot find <u>your</u> notes, you can always ask Piku for <u>his</u>.

9. He had finished <u>his</u> work, and so helped me to finish <u>mine</u>.

10. Is <u>your</u> name Rajiv? <u>Mine</u> is Raja and <u>his</u> is Gautam.

B. Point out the *nouns* the underlined *pronouns* or *possessive adjectives* refer to. One has been done for you.

Jayant said, 'I cannot walk to Delhi for <u>it</u> is too far away.'

Answer: **I** = Jayanta   **it** = Delhi

1. Mary asked Rita whether <u>she</u> had visited the new shop. Rita said that <u>she</u> had not even seen <u>it</u>.

2. Uncle Podger took the newspaper out of <u>his</u> bag and put <u>it</u> on the table.

3. Rinky told Piku, '<u>I</u> rang up Chandni last night and gave <u>her</u> <u>your</u> message.'

4. 'How can <u>you</u> be so foolish as to think that <u>I</u> shall lend you money!' Shylock told Antonio.

5. When Newton found that <u>his</u> dog Diamond had upset the lamp and burnt all his papers, <u>he</u> said, 'O Diamond! Diamond! <u>Thou</u> little knowest what thou hast done!'

6. Then Jesus told the lawyer, '<u>You</u> should act like the good Samaritan.'

7. The King was very angry that <u>he</u> had been deceived by the cunning thieves and wanted to punish <u>them</u>.

8. Simon told <u>his</u> brother, '<u>My</u> friends and I are going to the cinema. Would <u>you</u> like to come with <u>us</u>?'

9. The traveller asked Peter, 'Can <u>you</u> tell me where <u>I</u> can stay for the night?'

10. Gopalan went to <u>his</u> village when <u>he</u> heard that <u>his</u> friend was ill.

C. Fill in the blanks with *appropriate pronouns/words,* chosen from those given within brackets:

1. Where is John? Has anybody seen ....? *(he, him)*

2. While going to school, he met a friend of .... (him, his)

3. Sita said, 'We invited him, but he never came to that party of ....'
(ours, our)

4. This is a beautiful watch. Is it ....? (your, yours)

5. That is a lovely dress you are wearing. Where did you buy ....
from? (it, its)

6. I went to the zoo with some friends of .... (mine, my)

7. The dog was chasing .... own tail. (its, it's)

8. My mother often listens to this song. It's a favourite song of ....
(her, hers)

9. Gopalan said, 'Our flat is smaller than ....?' (their, theirs)

10. We know .... names, but they don't know .... (their/
theirs, our/ours)

D. Fill in the blanks with appropriate *pronouns* or *possessive adjectives*:

1. Ram's sister is a doctor. .... works in a hospital. She is married
to an engineer. .... husband works in a steel plant. ....
have a son. .... goes to a school near .... house.

2. Rita : How are ...., Susan? .... haven't seen you for a
long time.
Susan : My brother got married. So, ... went to Delhi to attend
.... wedding. .... came back from Delhi just yesterday.

3. John had a beautiful dog. ....
was golden brown in colour.
.... ears were long and
drooping. John gave .... away
to a cousin of .... when he
went to a boarding school.

4. Pratap: I can't find .... book.
Has anybody seen ....
anywhere?

Arka: .... is on the table. .... left it there when you went out last night.

Pratap: Thank ....

5. The cherry tree is famous for .... flowers. .... may be of different colours.

6. Peter doesn't like going to school. .... is always looking for some excuse to stay at home and play with .... model trains and toy soldiers. .... is, however, very good at studies and can do well with a little effort.

7. The little child was crying because .... had lost .... parents in the crowd at the temple. An old man picked it up in .... arms and tried to stop .... from crying.

8. 'Where can .... find a doctor to take care of my sick child?' asked the anxious mother. '......................... have to take .... to a hospital,' said the man.

9. The pilgrims lost all .... belongings when the bus .... were travelling in fell into a ravine.

10. The Giant did not let anybody enter his garden. So, when he saw the children playing in .... garden, ... was very angry.

11. 'Let .... go and play in the park,' said Raja to his friends.

12. Jayant: Why are .... limping, Ramen?

    Ramen: .... fell down and twisted my ankle.

13. Imran did not want to wear that shirt, for .... had a hole in ....

14. Did you and .... friends enjoy the picnic?

15. This is .... sweater and I shall put it on. Where is ....?
    .... should wear something warm. Look at the people all around. All of .... are wearing .... woollens.

Some More Adverbs

Adverbs of Degree

You have learnt than an adverb qualifies a verb.

> An adverb can also qualify (a) an *adjective* and (b) another *adverb*.

Adverbs Qualifying Adjectives

(a) This chair is **slightly** <u>smaller</u> than the other.

(b) That flower is **very** <u>beautiful</u>.

In (a), the adverb **slightly** tells us <u>how much</u> **smaller** this chair is compared to the other. The adverb **slightly**, therefore, qualifies the adjective **smaller**.

In (b), the adverb **very** tells us <u>how</u> **beautiful** that flower is, that is, the extent or degree of the flower's beauty. The adverb **very**, therefore, qualifies the adjective **beautiful**.

Adverbs Qualifying Adverbs

(a) Gopalan has worked **very** <u>hard</u>.

(b) Rinky answered the questions **pretty** <u>easily</u>.

In (a), the adverb **very** tells us <u>how</u> **hard** Gopalan has worked. The adverb **very**, therefore, modifies the adverb **hard**.

In (b), the adverb **pretty** tells us <u>how</u> **easily** Rinky answered the questions. The adverb **pretty**, therefore, modifies the adverb **easily**.

> Such adverbs, which answer the question (a) *how much?* or (b) *to what extent?* are known as ***adverbs of degree***.

One of the meanings of the word 'degree' is 'the amount or level' of something.

> Like other adverbs, adverbs of degree can also qualify *verbs*.

(a) We all <u>liked</u> our new teacher **immensely**. (**How much** did we **like** our new teacher?)

(b) He **absolutely** <u>refused</u> to listen to us. (**To what extent** did he **refuse** to listen to us?)

(c) Rita had **almost** <u>forgotten</u> to do her homework. (**To what extent** had Rita **forgotten** to do her homework?)

A. Pick out the *adverbs of degree* from the following sentences:

1. John had just closed the front door, when he remembered that he had simply forgotten to turn off the lights.

2. Jayant listened quite carefully to what Mahua said, but totally disagreed with her.

3. It was getting pretty dark, but we could see the house fairly clearly.

4. Ram said that he knew John far better than anybody else.

5. Madhu completely denied that she had said such a thing.

6. Though the bed was rather hard, I slept really well.

7. Tim is amazingly stupid, but unbelievably honest.

8. He was perfectly satisfied with the answers he received.

9. Rinky was terribly upset when she heard that Chandni was not coming to the party.

10. The children were truly delighted with the prizes they received.

Adverbs of Frequency

Look at these adverbs:

(a) Ram **always** <u>does</u> his work neatly.

(b) Javed **often** <u>does</u> his work neatly.

(c) John **sometimes** <u>does</u> his work neatly.

(d) Vimal **never** <u>does</u> his work neatly.

All these adverbs – **always, often, sometimes, never** – tell us **how often** or **frequently** something is **done** or **happens**.

Adverbs which tell us *how often* or *frequently* something happens or is done are known as ***adverbs of frequency***.

Do not confuse an ***adverb of time*** with an adverb of frequency. An adverb of time answers the question: **when?** An adverb of frequency answers the question: **how often?**

B. **Pick out the *adverbs of time* and *adverbs of frequency* from the following sentences:**

1. Yesterday Rita spoke to me twice on the phone.
2. Now that he has been warned, I am sure he will not misbehave again.
3. Roop often makes mistakes and is always sorry afterwards.
4. Peter has been told repeatedly to lock the door before he goes to sleep.
5. The pronouns 'thou', 'thee' and 'ye' are rarely used.
6. Arka sometimes stays up all night studying, but I never do so.
7. Jack has always been an obedient boy.
8. The library opens daily at 10 a.m.
9. John usually went home after school, but now he sometimes stays back to play with his friends.
10. 'I have seldom lied,' boasted Ramen.

Interrogative Adverbs

Adverbs, which are used to ask questions, are called ***interrogative adverbs***.

(a) **Why** was Roop late to school?   (**Why** here means **for what reason**.)

(b) **When** did John come home?   (**When** here means **at what time**.)

(c) **Where** does Jeff live?   (**Where** here means **at what place**.)

(d) **How** did the thief enter the house?   (**How** here means **in what way** or **manner**.)

Note that:

1. **How** can be used with other **adverbs**:

   How *fast* did he run?

   How *hard* has Gopalan worked?

   How *soon* can you come?

2. **How** can be used with **adjectives**:

   How *tall* is Ram?

   How *big* is the house?

   How *small* is the child?

3. **How** can be used with **much** and **many**:

   How *much* money did the thief steal?

   How *many* boys were present?

C. Fill in the blanks with suitable *interrogative adverbs*:

1. I cannot switch on this recorder. .... do you do it?

2. .... have you put the books? I have been looking for them all day.

3. I shall wait for you. .... will you be able to come?

4. .... many questions did Sam answer?

5. .... has John come so early? Nobody will come before evening.

6. .... important is the letter? Should I send it immediately?

7. I live in India. .... do you live?

8. .... cold is it outside? Should I wear a coat?

9. .... does the train arrive? Susan must be there to receive her friend.

10. .... was Jayant so tired? Has he been working all day?

11. .... have the pupils fared in the examination?

12. .... does she always look so angry?

Some More Adjectives

In Book 4, we looked at three kinds of adjectives: **qualitative**, **quantitative**, and **demonstrative**.

Quantitative Adjectives and Numerals

Quantitative adjectives tell us *how much* of a thing we are talking about:

(a) His success gave his parents **much** pleasure.

(b) Can you lend me **some** money?

(c) I have not been able to get any rest for the **whole** week.

When a quantitative adjective tells us *how many* persons or things we are talking about, some prefer to call it a ***numeral adjective***, or simply, a ***numeral***.

The two main kinds of numerals are:

(i) Definite Numeral Adjectives

Such an adjective mentions an exact or definite number:

(a) **Two** boys were walking down the road.

(b) Salim lent me **three** books.

(c) **ten** boys　　　　　(d) **forty** thieves　　　　　(e) **fifty** oranges

(ii) Indefinite Numeral Adjectives

Such adjectives tell us how many persons or things we are talking about without mentioning a definite number:

(a) There were **several** patients waiting to see the doctor.

(b) **Many** men died in that accident.

(c) We are sure that the work will be finished in a **few** days.

Note that an ordinary quantitative adjective just mentions a quantity and answers the question: **how much**?

An indefinite numeral adjective answers the question: **how many**? It does not, however, mention an exact number.

There are three kinds of **definite numeral adjectives**.

■ Such an adjective may be a definite number: *one, two, three* …and so on. It is then also known as a **cardinal**.

■ Such an adjective may describe the exact position or rank of a person or thing in a group or series:

(a) The **first** thing he did was to take off his shoes.

(b) The **third** goal was scored by the new player.

In (a), we are told that he did many things, the *first* of which was to take off his shoes. So, taking off his shoes was the **first in a series** of actions.

In (b), we learn that the goal scored by the new player was the **third in a series** of goals scored.

It is then also known as an **ordinal**.

■ Such an adjective may refer to a number less than one:

(a) Shyam worked for **half** a day.

(b) Kalyan bought the book for **one-third** its real price.

It is then also known as a **fraction**.

Interrogative Adjectives

The following are all **interrogative sentences**, that is, they ask questions:

(a) **Which** boy has broken the window?

(b) **What** gifts did you get on your birthday?

In sentence (a), **which** qualifies the noun **boy**.

In sentence (b), **what** qualifies the noun **gifts**.

Moreover, the words **which** and **what** have been used to ask **questions**.

When an adjective is used in this way to ask a question, it is called an *interrogative adjective*.

Emphasizing Adjectives

Sometimes, we use adjectives to **emphasize** what we want to say:

(a) What the man said was **absolute** rubbish.

(b) Sam was so shy that he stood at the **very** end of the line.

(c) The play was a **total** failure, for only a few people came to see it.

(d) John saw a tiger with his **own** eyes when he went to the jungle.

In sentence (a), the word **absolute** qualifies the noun **rubbish**. It has been used to emphasize the worthlessness of what the man said; it was not only rubbish, but **absolute** rubbish.

Similarly sentence (b) describes the extent of Sam's shyness: he not only stood at the end of the line, but at the **very** end of it. The word **very** qualifies the noun **end**.

Sentence (c) describes how great a failure the play was. It was not just a failure, it was a **total** failure. The word **total** qualifies the noun **failure**.

In sentence (d), the speaker wants to make it clear that what he/she says is true: John *did* see a tiger. So, he/she uses the word **own**, though it is not necessary, for the sake of emphasis. The word **own** qualifies the noun **eyes**.

Such an adjective is known as an *emphasizing adjective*.

Warning: Do not confuse an **emphasizing adjective** with an **adverb of degree**. An emphasizing adjective qualifies a <u>noun</u>, whereas an adverb of degree modifies a <u>verb</u>, an <u>adjective</u> or an <u>adverb</u>.

Pick out the *adjectives* from the following sentences and say of *what kind* each is:

1. We saw some pictures hanging on the bright walls of the room.
2. Which team is Suman playing for?
3. The first boy, who can answer the question, will receive a prize.
4. Ganesh has two brothers, and they are complete fools.
5. All members of the club are expected to donate fifty rupees.
6. What subject has Ranjit decided to study?
7. Rita repeated the exact words used by Pranati.
8. Have you read the story about Snow White and the seven dwarfs?
9. There were several people waiting to meet Mr Sen.
10. Srikant is an intelligent boy and can win the first prize.

Contractions

Sometimes, particularly when we are speaking or writing to friends or relatives, we shorten some English words by dropping one or more of the letters they are made up of. The shortened form is then joined to some other word that comes immediately before or after it. The word, which is shortened, and the word to which it is then added, are spoken or written as if they are one word.

When we do this while writing, we use a punctuation mark, called an **apostrophe,** in place of the missing letter or letters. An **apostrophe** looks like this: (**'**). It looks exactly like a closing inverted comma and is similarly written a little above the line.

A word, which is very often shortened or **contracted** like this, is the word '**not**' – we just drop the '**o**' and use the **apostrophe** in place of the '**o**'. Given below are some examples of this contraction:

is + **not** = is**n't**	does/do + **not** = does**n't**/do**n't**
are + **not** = are**n't**	was/were + **not** = was**n't**/were**n't**
can + **not** = ca**n't**	has/have + **not** = has**n't**/have**n't**

Each of these words – **isn't, doesn't, don't, aren't, wasn't, weren't, can't, hasn't, haven't** – is known as a **contraction,** for it contains fewer letters than the two original words it is made up of.

[The noun '**contraction**' is formed from the verb '**contract**', one of the meanings of which is 'to make something become less or smaller'.]

Note that when we do not use a contraction, we write or say:

(a) Why *is* John *not* coming to school?

(b) *Has* Raj *not* given you my message?

But when we use a contraction, we write or say:

(a) Why *isn't* John coming to school?

(b) *Hasn't* Raj given you my message?

Warning: You should not use contractions in formal written English: do not use contractions when writing examinations or doing your classwork or homework unless you have been specifically permitted to do so.

A. Rewrite the following sentences, replacing the underlined words with *contractions*:

1. Niti <u>does not</u> like strawberry jam.
2. That <u>is not</u> the book I wanted.
3. The boys <u>were not</u> paying attention in the class.
4. Bobby <u>was not</u> going to complain about his friends.
5. I <u>have not</u> got an extra ticket.
6. We <u>should not</u> tell lies.
7. Mickey <u>could not</u> tie his own shoelaces.
8. <u>Was</u> that not a moving story that he told us?
9. Arjun <u>did not</u> care if he was late.
10. Shyam <u>has not</u> come back home as yet.

Another word that is often contracted is the verb **is**. Given below are some examples of how it is contracted:

he + **is** = he**'s**	that + **is** = tha**t's**	she + **is** = she**'s**
what + **is** = what**'s**	who + **is** = who**'s**	where + **is** = where**'s**

In the words listed above, you will notice that the 'i' in **is** has been replaced by an apostrophe and the **'s** has been joined to another word.

Warning:

- You have to be careful about this **'s**, for the verb **has** is often contracted in the same way: the two letters '**ha**' are dropped and the **'s** is added to the previous word:

  he + **has** come = he**'s** come   John **has** gone = John**'s** gone

- In a sentence like '**John's** book is lying on the table', the **'s** is not the contracted form of the verb **is**. This apostrophe has been used to point out that the book <u>belongs</u> to John. The apostrophe, as used here, is a signal to denote **possession**.

(a) **Ritu's** sister is **Mahua's** friend.   (= sister of Ritu; = friend of Mahua)

(b) **Akash's** house is nearby.   (= house of Akash)

■ The contraction **it's** stands for **it is**:

(a) **It's** getting late.   (= It is)

(b) **It's** never too late to say sorry.   (= It is)

In the case of **it**, the apostrophe **s**, that is, the **'s**, is *never* used to denote possession. You should never use **it's** to mean something belonging to **it**:

Correct: The dog was wagging **its** tail.

Incorrect: The dog was wagging **it's** tail.

Correct: The bird flapped **its** wings.

Incorrect: The bird flapped **it's** wings.

B. Rewrite the following sentences, replacing the underlined words with *contractions*:

1. <u>She is</u> the girl who won the competition yesterday.

2. He <u>has not</u> got the key to the lock.

3. <u>Where is</u> the box full of sweets?

4. Ali <u>does not</u> like to get up early in the morning.

5. They <u>have not</u> won a single match so far.

6. Rana <u>was not</u> very sure about the answer.

7. <u>Who is</u> the man standing quietly in the corner?

8. I think <u>he is</u> the person we should speak to.

9. Sumita <u>could not</u> answer all the questions.

10. You <u>should not</u> make fun of people.

Some Frequently Used Contractions

The following is a list of some frequently used contractions:

shall not = **shan't**   should not = **shouldn't**

will not = **won't**   would not = **wouldn't**

did not = **didn't**   could not = **couldn't**

must not = **mustn't**   need not = **needn't**

I am = **I'm**   we are = **we're**

I have = **I've**   we have = **we've**

I will = **I'll**   we will = **we'll**

But note: **I'd** = I had **or** I would   **we'd** = we had **or** we would

Similarly,   **you'd** = you had/you would   **she'd** = she had/she would

             it'd = it had/it would   **they'd** = they had/they would

Note:

1. In questions and exclamations, **am not** is contracted to **aren't**:

    Aren't I right?   **Aren't** I playing today?

2. We can use **isn't, hasn't, haven't**, etc. at the end of a sentence, but we cannot use **'s, 've**, etc. in the same way:

    Correct: Do you know who *she is*?

    Incorrect: Do you know who *she's*?

3. Look at the question: 'Have you done your homework?'

    If the answer is: 'No, I **have not**,' it is **correct** to say: 'No, I **haven't**.'

    If the answer is: 'Yes, I **have**,' it is **incorrect** to say: 'Yes, **I've**.'

    You have to say: 'Yes, I **have**.'

4. Sometimes, two contractions are possible. We can say:

    (a) he **isn't** or **he's** not   (c) they **won't** or **they'll** not

    (b) you **aren't** or **you're** not

5. We can sometimes use a contraction after a noun:

    Rinky's an obedient girl.   (= Rinky is ....)

    His **mother's** ill.   (= His mother is ....)

6. We can use contractions with words like **who, where, how** in questions:

    (a) **who's** = who is/who has   (c) **where's** = where is/where has

    (b) **how's** = how is/how has

7. We can use contractions with **that, here, there** and **now** also.

C. Rewrite the following sentences without using any *contraction*:

1. 'Where's Ramen? I've got to speak to him immediately,' said Jayant.
   'Why, what's happened?' asked Piku.
   'My brother's fallen down and broken his leg.'

2. 'It's very warm today, isn't it?'
   'I really can't tell, for I've been sitting in this air-conditioned room all day.'
   'Aren't you lucky!'

3. 'How's your brother? Won't he play in today's match?'
   'No, he's busy – he's got to finish his homework.'
   'There's plenty of time. Today's only Saturday.'
   'I've tried to tell him that. It's no use.'

4. 'You're all young. Now's the time to look for adventure. You mustn't sit at home watching television all the time.'
   'We've got school tomorrow,' said Kalyan.
   'Kalyan's an idle fellow. Don't listen to him.'
   'He's right, you know. Who'll tell Ma that what we're looking for is adventure?'

5. 'You shouldn't have spoken to him like that.'
   'But aren't I right in telling him the truth?'
   'Truth's not pleasant. You mustn't forget that.'
   'Let's not talk about it anymore.'

D. Rewrite the following, using *contractions* wherever possible:

1. We had repeatedly warned him that he should not go there alone.
2. Chandan did not listen to us. He is now in trouble.
3. It is going to rain today. Where is your umbrella?
4. Shyam has come back. He could not get a ticket for the show.
5. Was I not right? You must not believe what he says.
6. Let us go to Roop's house. His mother is a good cook.
7. There is nothing to be afraid of. We are all here.
8. Sanjiv will not come today. He is not well.
9. Can you not hear the bell ringing?
10. 'I am going for a swim,' said Piku.

Rikki-Tikki-Tavi

Rikki-tikki was a mongoose. His eyes and the end of his nose were pink. He could scratch himself anywhere he pleased with any leg, back or front, and he could fluff up his tail until it looked like a bottle brush. His war-cry as he scuttled through the long grass was: rikk-tikk-tikki-tikki-tchk!

One day, a summer flood washed him out of the *burrow* where he lived and carried him down a roadside *ditch*. He found a little wisp of grass floating there, and clung to it till he lost his senses.

When he *revived*, he was lying in the hot sun in the middle of a garden path. A small boy and his mother took him into the house and a big man picked him up between his finger and thumb and said that he was not dead. So they wrapped him in cotton-wool and warmed him over a little fire, and he opened his eyes and sneezed.

It is the hardest thing in the world to frighten a mongoose, because he is full of *curiosity*.

They gave him a little piece of raw meat. Rikki-tikki liked it immensely, and when it was finished, he went out into the veranda and sat in the sunshine and fluffed up his fur to make it dry to the *roots*. Then he felt better. He spent all that day roaming all over the house. And when Teddy, the small boy, went to bed, Rikki-tikki climbed up, too. Teddy's mother and father came in to look at their son and saw Rikki-tikki on the *pillow*.

'I don't like that,' said Teddy's mother. 'He may bite the child.'
'He'll do no such thing,' said the boy's father. 'Teddy is safer with that little beast than if he had a *bloodhound* to watch over him.'

(Adapted from *Rikki-Tikki-Tavi* by Rudyard Kipling)

A. Read the passage and answer the following questions:

1. Who was Rikki-tikki? Describe him.
2. How do you think Rikki-tikki got his name?
3. Where did the summer flood carry Rikki-tikki?
4. How was he treated by the family who found him?
5. Why is it hard to frighten a mongoose?
6. What did Rikki-tikki eat and how did he dry himself completely?
7. What did Teddy's mother fear?
8. What did Teddy's father think?

B. Match each *word* with the *meaning* it has in the passage:

1. burrow	(i)	a large dog
2. ditch	(ii)	a strong desire to know or learn
3. revive	(iii)	a cushion to support the head
4. curiosity	(iv)	a hole made in the ground and used as a shelter by some animals
5. roots	(v)	to come back to consciousness
6. pillow	(vi)	those parts of hairs that attach the hairs to the body of a person or animal
7. bloodhound	(vii)	a long narrow channel dug at the edge of a field or road, etc. to carry water away

C. Pick out four *adjectives* from the passage. Mention of what *kind* each is and the *noun* it qualifies.

D. Pick out two *adverbs* from the passage. Mention of what *kind* each is and the word *(verb/adjective/adverb)* it qualifies.

E. Rewrite the following without using any *contraction*:

(a) 'I don't like that,' said Teddy's mother. 'He may bite the child.'

(b) 'He'll do no such thing,' said the boy's father. 'Teddy's safer with that little beast than if he'd a bloodhound to watch over him.'

Lost and Found

Harris was riding a bicycle with his wife through Holland. The roads were stony, and the machine jumped a good deal. 'Sit tight,' said Harris, without turning his head. Mrs Harris thought he said, 'Jump off.'

Mrs Harris did jump off, while Harris pedalled away hard thinking that she was still behind him. At first, she thought he was riding up the hill just to show off.

She expected him to jump off when he reached the top of the hill, and lean in a *careless* and *graceful* manner against the bicycle, waiting for her. When she saw him pass the top of the hill and cycle rapidly down the other side, she was quite *alarmed*. She ran to the top of the hill and shouted, but he never turned his head. She watched him *disappear* into a wood a mile and a half away, and then sat down and cried.

She had no money and she knew no Dutch. People passed, and seemed sorry for her. She tried to make them understand what had happened. They gathered that she had lost something, but could not *grasp* what. They took her to the nearest village, and found a policeman for her. From the signs she made, the policeman thought that some man had stolen her bicycle. They found a boy driving a lady's bicycle about four miles away. They brought him to her in a *cart*, but as Mrs. Harris did not want either him or his bicycle, they let him go again.

Meanwhile, Harris continued his ride with much enjoyment. It seemed to him that he had suddenly become a stronger cyclist. 'I haven't felt this machine so light for months. It's this air, I think. It's doing me good,' he said. Then he told his wife not to be afraid, and he would show her how fast he could go.

He *sped* merrily on for about five miles. Then, the feeling began to grow upon him that something was wrong. He stretched out his hand behind him and felt: there was nothing there. He jumped, or rather fell off, and looked back up the road. It stretched white and straight and not a living soul could be seen on it.

Harris was in a *panic*. He asked several people, but nobody could understand anything that he was saying except that he seemed to have lost a lady. A young man suggested the police station at the next town. Harris made his way there.

The police gave him a piece of paper, and told him to write down a full description of his wife, together with the details of when and where he had lost her. He did not know where he had lost her – all he could tell them was the name of the village where he had had his lunch. He knew he had her with him then, and they had started from there together.

With the help of a hotel-keeper, who spoke a little English, the police were able to make out what he wanted. In the evening they brought her to him in a covered *wagon*, together with a bill of *expenses*. She was very angry!

(Adapted from *Three Men on the Bummel* by Jerome K. Jerome)

A. Read the passage and answer the following questions:

1. Why did Mrs Harris jump off the bicycle?
2. What did Mrs Harris think her husband was doing?
3. Why could people not grasp what Mrs Harris was trying to tell them?

4. What did the policeman understand from the signs that Mrs Harris made? What did the police do as a result?
5. Why did Mr Harris enjoy his ride so much more?
6. What was all the information that Mr Harris was able to give the police about where he had lost his wife?
7. How was Mrs Harris finally brought to Mr Harris?

B. Tick the *meaning* each of the following *words* has in the passage:

1. careless
   (i) a gentle touch
   (ii) a person who looks after the sick
   (iii) without attention and thought

2. graceful
   (i) showing a pleasing beauty in movement and manner
   (ii) kind, polite and generous
   (iii) not attractive or elegant

3. alarmed
   (i) a clock which rang
   (ii) felt anxious or afraid
   (iii) felt sorry

4. disappear
   (i) to prevent an action from taking place
   (ii) to fail to be interesting
   (iii) to vanish from sight

5. grasp
   (i) to work hard
   (ii) to understand fully
   (iii) to struggle

6. cart
   (i) a suitcase
   (ii) a vehicle with two or four wheels, usually pulled by a horse
   (iii) a map or drawing

7. sped
   (i) moved quickly
   (ii) gave money for something
   (iii) a small wild plant

8. panic   (i) a sudden sharp feeling of pain

                           (ii) a feeling of great fear that cannot be controlled

                       (iii) an outing with a party

9. wagon   (i) to move from side to side

                           (ii) a small bird with a long tail

                       (iii) a vehicle on four wheels, usually pulled by horses or oxen

10. expenses   (i) gaining knowledge or skill

                           (ii) money spent in doing or buying something

                       (iii) costing a lot of money

C. Say what kind of an *adjective* or *adverb* each of the underlined words is:

1. He leaned in a <u>graceful</u> manner against the bicycle.

2. She was <u>quite</u> alarmed.

3. They took her to the <u>nearest</u> village.

4. <u>Meanwhile</u>, Harris continued his ride with <u>much</u> enjoyment.

5. He sped <u>merrily</u> on for about <u>five</u> miles.

D. Pick out the *personal pronouns* from the following sentences and in each case mention its *person*:

1. She had no money and she knew no Dutch. People passed and seemed sorry for her. She tried to make them understand what had happened. They gathered that she had lost something.

2. 'I <u>haven't</u> felt this machine so light for months. <u>It's</u> this air, I think. <u>It's</u> doing me good,' he said.

E. Rewrite the sentences in Ex. D. 2, using the full forms of the underlined *contractions*.

F. Show how each of the following words has been formed with the help of a *prefix* or *suffix*. An example has been given to help you.

Example: rapidly = rapid + –ly

jumped, careless, graceful, disappear, nearest, stronger, feeling

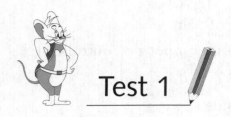

Test 1

A. Point out the *prefix* and/or *suffix* used in each of the underlined words. Two examples have been given to help you.

   (a) Sumit is unwell.   Answer: unwell = **un–** + well

   (b) This toy is unbreakable. Answer. unbreakable = **un–** + break + **–able**

1. Mahatma Gandhi believed in non-violence.
2. The manager told us that the hotel was full.
3. That man is dishonest and totally unreliable.
4. Srinath was unhappy that we had misunderstood him.
5. Mahua has countless stories to tell, but none of them is believable.

B. Complete the following table:

personal pronoun	I	…………	she	…………	it	…………	they
reflexive form	…………	yourselves	…………	ourselves	…………	yourself	…………

C. Fill in the blanks with appropriate *adverbs* or *adjectives*:

1. I tried ……………… hard to finish the work in time.
2. Nobody could guess who the thief was till the ……………… end of the story.
3. ……………… did you go home last night?
4. ……………… train takes the least time to go from here to Delhi?
5. Madhu is ……………… absent from school and always gets the prize for best attendance.
6. Has the doctor given you ……………… medicine for your fever?
7. The teacher said, 'Can those, sitting on the ……………… bench, hear me?'
8. ……………… much time have you wasted doing nothing?
9. It was bitterly ……………… and we all crowded round the fire.

10. .... are you still lying in bed? Are you ill?

D. Rewrite the following, using *contractions* wherever possible:

1. Ram has not as yet told me that he is not coming this evening.
2. Where is the gift that you said that you would buy me?
3. Should you not tell Rita that she is getting too fat?
4. 'You are a very intelligent boy. I am going to give you a prize,' said the teacher.
5. Raj did not know what to do; he could not tell Kaushik that he had lost the book.

E. Fill in the blanks with correct forms of *pronouns*:

1. Though Bharti does not eat fish ...., she does not mind cooking .... for us.
2. Say only what .... yourself have heard. Do not spread rumours.
3. The boys made all the arrangements for this picnic by .... and .... was very enjoyable. .... should be congratulated.
4. Vimal said, 'I do not worry about .... It is this brother of .... who worries me.'
5. These children cannot look after .... We must look after ....
6. Vinod has borrowed a book of .... I have to ask .... to return it, for I want to read ....
7. Though he does not know how to read and write ...., Govinda has set up a school in his village.
8. Speak for .... You do not have to speak for .... We can take care of ....
9. All of them wanted something for ....
10. Each man must protect ...., who does not, may lose his life.

F. Punctuate the following:

the man told sushil i want to meet your father he is not at home replied sushil when will he come back asked the man i dont know replied sushil

39

Verbs of Incomplete Predication

You know that verbs may be **transitive** or **intransitive**.

1. A verb, which **has an object**, is a *transitive* verb.

(a) Ram **bought** a book.

[Question: Ram **bought** what/whom? Answer: (a) <u>book</u>

Secondly, <u>book</u> refers to something that is different and distinct from **Ram**, the subject. Therefore, <u>book</u> is the object of the verb **bought**.]

In this sentence, the verb **bought** is transitive because it has an object *book*.

2.   A verb, which **does not have an object**, is an *intransitive* verb.

(b) Rita **sang**.

[Question: Rita sang what/whom? No answer.]

In this sentence, the verb **sang** is intransitive because it has no object.

(c) Kalyan **is** a musician.

[Question: Kalyan is what/whom?   Answer. (a) <u>musician</u>

But, <u>musician</u> refers to Kalyan himself. It does not refer to somebody or something different or distinct from the subject, **Kalyan**. Therefore, <u>musician</u> is not an object of the verb **is**.]

The verb *is* in this sentence has no object and is an intransitive verb.

Verbs of Incomplete Predication

Now look at these sentences:

(d) Rita **sang**.

(e) The boy **seems** <u>happy</u>.

(f) Ashoka **was** <u>a great emperor</u>.

(g) Kumar **looks** <u>very ill</u>.

In (d), the verb **sang** is intransitive, but what it says about **Rita** makes complete sense: no other word is needed to make the sense complete.

In (e), the verb **seems** is also intransitive, but what it says about the **boy** will not make complete sense if we omit the word <u>happy</u>:

The boy **seems** .... (what?)

A word, like <u>happy</u>, <u>sad</u>, or <u>cheerful</u>, is needed to make the sense complete.

Similarly in (f), the intransitive verb **was** needs the words <u>a great emperor</u> to complete what it says about **Ashoka**.

In (g), the intransitive verb **looks** needs the words <u>very ill</u> to complete what it says about **Kumar**.

3. (i) An **intransitive verb**, which needs the help of some word or words to complete what it says about the <u>subject</u>, is called a *verb of incomplete predication*.

   (ii) The word or group of words which helps the verb to <u>complete</u> what it says is known as the *complement*.

   [The meaning of the word **complement** here is 'something which helps to *complete* another thing'.]

   (iii) Since such a complement helps the verb to complete what it says about its <u>subject</u>, it is known as a *subjective complement*.

4. A **transitive** verb may also need a complement:

   (h) The people **made** *Rama* <u>king</u>.

   Question: The people **made** what/whom (king)? Ans. *Rama*

   Secondly, *Rama* refers to somebody different from the subject, **people**.

   Therefore, *Rama* is the object of the verb **made**.

   But, if the word **king** is left out, the sentence will not make complete sense:

   The people **made** *Rama* .... (what?)

   The word <u>king</u> is needed to complete what the verb **made** says about its object, *Rama*.

(i) I **found** the *story* <u>quite interesting</u>.

Question: I **found** what/whom (interesting)? Ans. (the) *story*

Secondly, *story* refers to something different from **I**, the subject.

So, *story* is the object of the verb **found**.

But, the words <u>quite interesting</u> are needed to complete what the verb **found** says about its object, *story*.

5. (i) A **transitive verb**, which needs the help of some word or words to complete what it says about its <u>object</u>, is called a ***verb of incomplete predication***.

(ii) The word or group of words which helps the verb to <u>complete</u> what it says is known as the ***complement***.

(iii) Since such a complement helps the verb to complete what it says about its <u>object</u>, it is known as an ***objective complement***.

Summary

1. A verb may be **transitive** or **intransitive**.

2. Some transitive and intransitive verbs require a word or words (a **complement**) to help them *complete* what they say. Such verbs, transitive or intransitive, are known as **verbs of incomplete predication**.

   Verbs like **be**, **become**, **seem**, **appear** and those which express the same ideas are usually **verbs of incomplete predication**.

3. If the complement tells us something about the subject, it is known as a **subjective complement**.

   Intransitive verbs take subjective complements.

4. If the complement tells us something about the object, it is known as an **objective complement**.

   Transitive verbs take objective complements.

Warning

There may be some confusion between a transitive verb of incomplete predication and a transitive verb with two objects: *direct* and *indirect*.

(j) Ram **found** <u>Hari</u> asleep.

(k) Ram **found** <u>Hari</u> <u>a place to stay</u>.

Let us look at example (j) first.

Question: Ram **found** what/whom? Ans. <u>Hari</u>

Secondly, <u>Hari</u> refers to a person different from Ram. So, <u>Hari</u> is the object of the verb **found**.

But, the word <u>asleep</u> does not answer any of the questions: what/whom?

Secondly, <u>asleep</u> refers to Hari, the object, and without it the sentence does not make complete sense. The word is helping the verb **found** to complete what it says about the object, <u>Hari</u>.

So, **asleep** is an objective complement.

At first sight, example (k) seems to be similar to (j). Without the words 'a place to stay', the sentence does not make sense:

Ram found Hari .... (what?)

Remember, however, we must first find the verb, then the subject and then see whether the verb has any object or objects.

So, let us look at sentence (k) carefully:

Ram **found** what/whom?   what?   Ans. <u>place</u>

                                                whom?   Ans. <u>Hari</u>

Note that <u>Hari</u> and <u>place</u> are different and separate from the subject, **Ram**. Also, <u>Hari</u> and <u>place</u> are different from each other.

So, they are both objects of the verb **found**. <u>Hari</u> is the indirect object and <u>place</u>, the direct object.

In (j), however, **asleep** describes the object itself: it is not something that can be separated from the object.

Remember that an objective complement tells us something about the object itself, whereas a direct object and an indirect object refer to two separate things or persons and one does not describe the other.

Say which of the *verbs* in the following sentences are *transitive* and which *intransitive*. Point out the *objects* of transitive verbs and the *complements* of verbs of incomplete predication. Remember that a transitive verb may have two objects: *direct* and *indirect*.

1. The room was dark and cool.
2. The teacher made Piku the monitor of the class.
3. After a long rest, Ramen felt fresh and energetic.
4. In the morning, we found him asleep in the garden.
5. The members of the club elected him President.
6. Reena closed the door of the room.
7. Sachin has become a doctor.
8. Ram taught me mathematics.
9. John wrote Jeff a long letter.
10. Vinay called Govinda a liar.
11. The boxer knocked his opponent senseless.
12. Everybody blamed him.
13. I feel a bit of a fool.
14. He has always been a loyal friend.
15. John will be a good captain of the team.
16. Milly looked happy and relieved.
17. Sujit called Arka a genius.
18. The travellers seemed tired and hungry.
19. The weak child has grown healthy and strong.
20. The food smelt delicious.
21. Over the phone, Chandan sounded sad.
22. The lemonade tasted flat and bitter.
23. The parents called their child 'Rishi.'
24. On Ramen's birthday, I gave him a book and some flowers.
25. The sun gives the earth heat and light.

Sentences, Phrases and Clauses

10

The Sentence

You know that a *sentence* is a group of words (i) which contains a **subject** and a **predicate**, and (ii) which makes <u>complete sense</u> by itself, that is, it does not depend on any other word or group of words to do so.

Since a **predicate** must contain a *verb*, it follows that a *sentence* must contain a **subject** and a *verb*.

Remember that a **predicate** may be made up of only a *verb*.
- (a) The **king** <u>sat on a throne of gold</u>.
- (b) The **party** <u>will be held at sunset</u>.
- (c) **Rita** <u>was reading a book of poems</u>.

Each of the above groups of words contains a **subject** and a **predicate**:

- (a) **king** (subject)   +   sat on a throne of gold (predicate)
- (b) **party** (subject)   +   will be held at sunset (predicate)
- (c) **Rita** (subject)   +   was reading a book of poems (predicate)

Also, each makes complete sense by itself. So, all three are *sentences*.

The Phrase

Now look at the sentences again. They contain smaller groups of words, none of which contains a subject and a predicate:

(a) **of gold**   (b) **at sunset**   (c) **of poems**

Moreover, none of these makes complete sense by itself: each depends on other groups of words to do so. Such a group of words is known as a *phrase*.

For the present, we shall define a *phrase* as a group of words which does not contain a subject and a predicate, and does not make complete sense by itself.

The Clause

(d) The **king** <u>sat on a throne</u>. (e) The **throne** <u>was made of gold</u>.

First, in (d) there is a subject **king** and a predicate: *sat on a throne*, and in (e) there is a subject **throne**, and a predicate: *was made of gold*.

Secondly, each makes complete sense by itself. So, each is a sentence.

If we now join these two sentences, we get:

The king sat on a throne and the throne was made of gold.

Since the two sentences have become parts of a larger sentence, we do not call them 'sentences' any longer. We call them *clauses*.

For the present, we shall define a *clause* as a group of words, which contains a subject and a predicate, and is a part of a sentence.

Let us take two more examples:

(f) The party will be held **when the sun sets**.
(g) **While she was waiting for the train**, Rita was reading a book of poems.

In (f), there are two clauses: (i) <u>The party will be held</u>, and (ii) <u>when the sun sets</u>. In (g), there are two clauses: (i) <u>While she was waiting for the train</u>, and (ii) <u>Rita was reading a book of poems</u>.

Phrases and Clauses

(a) The queen wore a *diamond* crown.
(b) The queen wore a crown *of diamonds*.
(c) The queen wore a crown *which was made of diamonds*.

In (a), **diamond** is an *adjective* qualifying the noun 'crown'.

In (b), **of diamonds**, which does not contain a subject and a predicate, is a *phrase* that qualifies the noun 'crown'.

In (c), **which was made of diamonds**, which consists of a subject 'which' and a predicate: *was made of diamonds*, is a *clause* that qualifies the noun 'crown'.

(d) Ram answered the question *immediately*.
(e) Ram answered the question *without any delay*.

In (d), **immediately** is an *adverb* that qualifies the verb 'answered'.

In (e), **without any delay**, which does not contain a subject and a predicate, is a *phrase* which qualifies the verb 'answered'.

(f) The girl with a *smiling* face is my sister.

(g) The girl *with a smile on her face* is my sister.

(h) The girl, *who is smiling*, is my sister.

(i) *When the girl smiles*, she looks beautiful.

In (f), **smiling** is an *adjective* which qualifies the noun 'face'.

In (g), **with a smile on her face**, which does not contain a subject and a predicate, is a *phrase* which qualifies the noun 'girl'.

In (h), **who is smiling**, which contains a subject 'who' and a predicate: *is smiling*, is a *clause* which qualifies the noun 'girl'.

In (i), there are two *clauses*: (1) girl (subject) + smiles (predicate); (2) she (subject) + looks beautiful (predicate); 'when' is a *conjunction* joining the two *clauses*.

What is to be noted is that *clause* (1) does the work of an *adverb* which qualifies the verb 'looks' in *clause* (2).

Say which of the underlined groups of words are *phrases* and which *clauses*:

  1. The boy, who was ill, lay on a bed in the hospital.
  2. The girl was wearing a chain of gold and shoes that were made of leather.
  3. What you have said is not correct.
  4. John met Robert, who was carrying a big bag, in the market.
  5. The travellers, who were hungry and tired, wanted to go to a hotel without any further delay.
  6. Piku, a good swimmer, swam easily across the lake.
  7. The boy, who had won the race, was given a crown of laurel leaves.
  8. After he returned from Mumbai, Ramen fell ill.
  9. The Principal heard everything the students wanted to say with patience.
  10. The man, who was injured in the accident, was admitted to a hospital near his house.

Kinds of Phrases

A phrase is a group of words that does not contain a subject and a predicate. We shall now look at three different kinds of phrases:

1. **adjective** phrases   2. **adverb** phrases   3. **noun** phrases

Adjective Phrases

A phrase, which does the work of an adjective, is an *adjective phrase*.

(a) The king sat on a throne **of gold**. (b) We saw a bird **with a long beak**.

In (a), the phrase **of gold** describes the noun **throne**. So, **of gold** is an adjective phrase. It is made up of: **of** (preposition) + **gold** (noun).

In (b), the phrase **with a long beak** describes the noun **bird**. So, **with a long beak** is an adjective phrase. It is made up of: **with** (preposition) + **a** (article) + **long** (adjective) + **beak** (noun).

So, it does not matter what the phrase is made up of. What matters is the **work** it does in a clause or a sentence.

Remember that the **–ing** form of a verb, which is also called the **present participle**, may act as an **adjective** and can be used to make up a phrase:

  (a) The *speeding* car crashed against a tree.

  (b) A car, *running at high speed*, crashed against a tree.

In (a), **speeding** has been used as a simple adjective to qualify 'car'.

[Q: What kind of a car? Ans: speeding]

In (b), **running at high speed** does not contain a subject and a predicate. It is, therefore, a phrase, in which the **–ing** form of the verb 'run' has been used to describe the noun 'car'.

[Q: What kind of a car?   Ans: running at high speed]

'Running at high speed' is, therefore, an adjective phrase qualifying 'car'.

Warning: When you come across the **–ing** form of a verb, what you must try to find out is whether it is being used as an adjective or as a main verb with the assistance of a helping verb. Remember that the **–ing** form of a verb cannot act as a verb without the help of another verb.

Let us look at another example:

(c) The girl, *picking flowers*, is my sister.

In (c), **picking flowers** does not contain a subject and a predicate. So, it is a **phrase**. The phrase describes the noun 'girl.' So, it is an adjective phrase that contains an **–ing** form of a verb (pick + **–ing**) acting like an adjective.

[In a sentence like 'A girl *is picking* flowers,' **picking** is a verb = 'is' (helping verb) + **–ing** = **picking**, the *present continuous tense* of the verb 'pick.']

A. Pick out the *adjective phrases* from the following sentences:

1. The girl with blue eyes is my sister.
2. The flowers in the garden were very beautiful.
3. We saw a tiger drinking at a waterhole.
4. The students were asked to wear dresses of the same colour.
5. Sita kept her bag, full of books, on the table.
6. The water, glistening in the light of the moon, looked like silver.
7. The soldier was honoured for his act of extraordinary courage.
8. The boys were playing with marbles of glass.
9. They saw an old lady, carrying a basket full of ripe apples.
10. Please give me that book lying on the table.
11. There were two dogs, of the same breed, near the gate.
12. They found it difficult to walk along the path full of potholes and mud.
13. These books, dealing with mathematical problems, belong to Raj.
14. The sun, setting in a blaze of colours, lit up the landscape.
15. That man with a moustache is a famous actor.

Adverb Phrases

A phrase, which does the work of an adverb, is an *adverb phrase*.

(a) Shyam does all his work **with great care**.

(b) John will be here **in an hour**.

(c) You can get this book **in all the bookshops**.

In (a), **with great care**, which does not contain a subject and a predicate, tells us **how** Shyam does his work. So, **with great care** is an adverb phrase (manner).

In (b), **in an hour**, which also does not have a subject and a predicate, tells us **when** John will come. So, **in an hour** is an adverb phrase (time).

In (c), **in all the bookshops** does not contain a subject and a predicate. It tells us **where** the book is available, and so it is an adverb phrase (place).

B. Pick out the *adverb phrases* from the following sentences:

1. The king treated his defeated enemy with great kindness.
2. John was shouting at the top of his voice.
3. The children were playing in the Selfish Giant's garden.
4. The visitor rang the bell again and again, but nobody opened the door.
5. The old man was weak and could only speak in a whisper.
6. Salim left the house in a hurry and forgot to take his bag.
7. There were at least five hundred people in the two buildings.
8. Even after a long discussion, they failed to come to a decision.
9. There were pieces of glass all over the floor.
10. Kalyan tried to push the door open with all his strength.
11. The players tried heart and soul to win the match.
12. Examinations are held in our school every week.
13. Piku put all his luggage in the boot of the car.
14. The guard stood near the door and kept a careful watch.
15. The doctor told him to take the pills three times a day.

Noun Phrases

A phrase, which does the work of a noun, is a **noun phrase**.

Remember that only a noun or pronoun (a substitute for a noun), or a group of words acting like a noun can be the <u>subject</u> or <u>object</u> of a verb. So, a phrase, which is the subject or object of a verb, is a **noun phrase**.

(a) *Getting up early in the morning* **is** a good habit.

    Getting up early in the morning does not contain a subject and a predicate.

So it is a **phrase**. *Getting up early in the morning* is the **subject** of the verb **is**. It is, therefore, a noun phrase.

[Q: What is a good habit? Ans: *Getting up early in the morning*]

(b) Robert **enjoys** *listening to music*.

[Q: What does Robert enjoy? Ans: *listening to music*]

In (b), *listening to music* is the **object** of the verb **enjoys**. As it does not contain a subject and a predicate, it is a phrase acting like a noun, or a noun phrase.

C. Pick out the *noun phrases* from the following sentences:

1. Rinky enjoys reading ghost stories.
2. Jayant does not like eating vegetarian food.
3. Mahua told us all about the burglary.
4. Writing an interesting letter is an art.
5. Ratna knows everybody's secrets.
6. Remembering people's names and addresses is not easy.
7. Piku fed all the local street dogs every day.
8. I hate working on a Sunday.
9. Susan has forgotten her appointment with the dentist.
10. Looking at the stars in the sky fills us with wonder and awe.
11. A scientist carefully notes down all experimental observations.
12. Shyam's conduct at the meeting was shameful.
13. The Indians wanted their freedom from foreign rule.
14. All the passengers of the train were angry at the delay.
15. Children love going on a picnic.

Kinds of Sentences and Clauses

A group of words that contains a subject and a predicate and makes complete sense by itself is a **sentence**.

A group of words that contains a subject and a predicate, and is a part of a sentence is a **clause**.

Kinds of Clauses

1. A sentence may consist of **one** or **more than one** clause:
   (a) The puppy was playing with a ball.
   (b) The puppy was playing with a ball which was made of rubber.

   Sentence (a) contains only one subject (*puppy*) and one predicate: *was playing with a ball* (verb: was playing).

   Sentence (a), therefore, contains only one clause.

   Sentence (b), however, contains two clauses:
   (i) The puppy was playing with a ball
       [subject: *puppy*; predicate: *was playing with a ball* (verb: was playing)]
   (ii) which was made of rubber
       [subject: *which*; predicate: *was made of rubber* (verb: was made)]

   Note that clause (i) makes complete sense by itself, but clause (ii) does not. Clause (ii) is an adjective clause that qualifies the noun 'ball'.
   We call clause (i) the **main** or **principal** clause.
   We call clause (ii) a **dependent** or **subordinate** clause, because it depends on clause (i) to make sense.
   [The word **dependent** means something which '*depends on*' another thing. The word **subordinate** means something which is '*of less importance*' than another thing.]

2. A sentence may contain two or more **main** or **principal** clauses:
   (c) Arka lives in Kolkata and I live in Delhi.

This sentence contains two clauses:

 (i) Arka lives in Kolkata

   [subject: *Arka*; predicate: *lives in Kolkata* (verb: lives)]

(ii) I live in Delhi

   [subject: *I*; predicate: *live in Delhi* (verb: live)]

The two clauses are joined by the conjunction **and**.

Note that each clause makes complete sense by itself.

Such clauses, which are parts of the same sentence and each of which makes complete sense by itself, are known as *coordinate clauses*.

[The word **coordinate** here means '*equal in importance or rank*'.]

Kinds of Sentences

1. A *sentence* may consist of just **one clause**.

   (a) Arka lives in Kolkata.

   [subject: *Arka*; predicate: *lives in Kolkata* (verb: *lives*)]

   Such a sentence is known as a *simple* sentence.

2. A *sentence* may contain **one main clause**, and **one or more than one subordinate clause**.

   (b) Arka, who is my friend, lives in Kolkata.

   This sentence contains **two** clauses:

    (i) Arka lives in Kolkata [subject: *Arka*; predicate: *lives in Kolkata* (verb: *lives*)]

   (ii) who is my friend [subject: *who*; predicate: *is my friend* (verb: *is*)]

   Clause (i) makes complete sense by itself.

   Clause (ii) does not make complete sense by itself.

   So, clause (i) is the *main* or *principal* clause, and clause (ii) is a *dependent* or *subordinate* clause.

   (c) Arka, who is my friend, bought a car, which was white in colour.

   This sentence contains **three** clauses:

    (i) Arka bought a car [subject: *Arka*; predicate: *bought a car* (verb: *bought*)]

   (ii) who is my friend [subject: *who*; predicate: *is my friend* (verb: *is*)]

   (iii) which was white in colour [subject: *which*; predicate: *was white in colour* (verb: *was*)]

Clause (i) makes complete sense by itself.

None of the clauses (ii) and (iii) makes complete sense by itself.

So clause (i) is the **main** or **principal** clause, and clauses (ii) and (iii) are *subordinate* clauses.

Such a *sentence*, which consists of **one main clause** and **one or more than one subordinate clause**, is called a *complex* sentence.

3.   A *sentence* may contain **two or more** independent or **coordinate clauses**.

(d) The ground was slippery and I fell down.

This sentence contains **two** clauses:

 (i) The ground was slippery [subject: *ground*; predicate: *was slippery* (verb: *was*)]

(ii) I fell down [subject: *I*; predicate: *fell down* (verb: *fell*)]

The clauses are joined to each other by the conjunction: **and**.

Each clause makes complete sense by itself.

They are, therefore, *coordinate clauses*.

(e) The ground was slippery and I fell down, but Ram helped me up.

This sentence contains **three** clauses:

 (i) The ground was slippery [subject: *ground*; predicate: *was slippery* (verb: *was*)]

(ii) I fell down [subject: *I*; predicate: *fell down* (verb: *fell*)]

(iii) Ram helped me up [subject: *Ram*; predicate: *helped me up* (verb: *helped*)]

The clauses are joined by the conjunctions: **and, but**.

Each clause makes complete sense by itself. So, all three are *coordinate clauses*.

Such a *sentence*, which contains **two or more coordinate clauses**, is known as a *compound* sentence.

Some call a compound sentence consisting of <u>two</u> coordinate clauses a *double* sentence, and a compound sentence consisting of <u>more than two</u> coordinate clauses a *multiple* sentence.

4. A *sentence* may consist of **two or more coordinate clauses**, and **one or more than one subordinate clause**.

   (f) Arka, who is my friend, lives in Kolkata and Ram, who is also a friend of mine, lives in Mumbai.

The sentence consists of **four** clauses:

  (i) Arka lives in Kolkata [subject: *Arka*; predicate: *lives in Kolkata* (verb: *lives*)]

  (ii) who is my friend [subject: *who*; predicate: *is my friend* (verb: *is*)]

 (iii) Ram lives in Mumbai [subject: *Ram*; predicate: *lives in Mumbai* (verb: *lives*)]

 (iv) who is also my friend [subject: *who*; predicate: *is also my friend* (verb: *is*)]

Each of the clauses (i) and (iii) makes complete sense by itself.

None of the clauses (ii) and (iv) makes complete sense by itself.

So, clauses (i) and (iii) are *coordinate clauses*, and clauses (ii) and (iv) are *subordinate clauses*.

The two coordinate clauses are joined by the conjunction: **and**.

A *sentence*, which consists of *two or more coordinate clauses* and *one or more than one subordinate clause*, is called a *compound-complex* sentence.

Kinds of Clauses

We shall now look at three kinds of **subordinate** clauses:

1. **adjective** clauses   2. **adverb** clauses   3. **noun** clauses

Adjective Clauses

A subordinate clause, which does the work of an adjective, is an *adjective clause*.

(a) The thief, *who stole the jewels*, has been caught.

(b) He killed a snake, *which was highly poisonous*.

In (a), *who stole the jewels* is a clause.

[subject: *who*; predicate: *stole the jewels* (verb: *stole*)]

It qualifies the noun **thief**. It is, therefore, an *adjective clause*.

In (b), *which was highly poisonous* is a clause.

[subject: *which*; predicate: *was highly poisonous* (verb: *was*)]

It qualifies the noun **snake**. It is, therefore, an *adjective clause*.

A. Pick out the *adjective clauses* from the following sentences and mention the *nouns* they qualify:

1. Sushanta bought the book which you liked so much.
2. The boy, who rescued the baby from the fire, became the hero of the locality.
3. My friend, who is a doctor, lives nearby.
4. The storm, which destroyed the village, lasted for three days.
5. The house, which his father built, is now a hospital.
6. John saw the accident in which so many people were killed.
7. Did you watch the match which was won by New Zealand?
8. A man, who is kind and generous, is liked by everybody.
9. Who is that man who is standing near the gate?
10. The boy, who wins the race, will get a prize.

Adverb Clauses

A subordinate clause, which does the work of an adverb, is an *adverb clause*.

(a) The car <u>was found</u> *where the accident took place.*

(b) I <u>entered</u> the room *just when John came in.*

In (a), *where the accident took place* is a clause.

[subject: *accident*; predicate: *where, took place* (verb: *took place*)]

It is an *adverb clause* of place which tells us <u>where</u> the car <u>was found</u>. It, therefore, qualifies the verb **was found** in the main clause.

In (b), *just when John came in* is a clause.

[subject: *John*; predicate: *just when, came in* (verb: *came*)]

It tells us more about the time <u>when I entered</u>. It is, therefore, an *adverb clause* of time that qualifies the verb **entered** in the main clause.

B. Pick out the *adverb clauses* from the following sentences:

1. Ram will go home when he has finished all his tasks.
2. The train left just as we entered the station.
3. Shyam has kept his money where it will be safe.
4. Park your car where we can see it.
5. Before he sat down, Jayant closed the door.
6. 'You can sit wherever you like,' Chandan said.
7. Please call us whenever you need any help.
8. Plant the seed where there is sunlight and air.
9. It is no use being sorry after you have done something in a hurry.
10. The tree bore flowers when spring came.

Noun Clauses

A clause, which does the work of a noun, is a **noun clause**.

Only a noun, or a word or group of words that does the work of a noun can be the **subject** or **object** of a verb.

(a) *What John said* <u>surprised</u> everybody

(b) Please <u>tell</u> me *what happened last night*.

In (a), *What John said* is a clause.

[subject: *John*; predicate: *What, said* (verb: *said*)]

Secondly, it is the **subject** of the verb **surprised** in the main clause.

[Q: *What* surprised everybody? Ans: *What John said*]

It is, therefore, a **noun clause**.

In (b), *what happened last night* is a clause.

[subject: *what*; predicate: *happened last night* (verb: *happened*)]

It is the **direct object** of the verb **tell** in the main clause.

[Q: Please tell me *what*? Ans: *what happened last night*]

It is, therefore, a **noun clause**.

[Note that **me** is the indirect object of the verb **tell**.]

C. Pick out the *noun clauses* from the following sentences:

1. I cannot believe that Kalyan has done such a thing.
2. Everybody knew that Ram was going to Delhi.

3. That the earth goes round the sun is a fact.
4. Whoever has stolen the money is bound to be caught.
5. Nobody can say what will happen in the future.
6. Why Mahua suddenly became so angry is a mystery.
7. Our teacher told us that Shakespeare was a great dramatist.
8. You should watch what the dog does.
9. The man wrote down the message I gave him.
10. Whether Ramen would come was uncertain.

D. Pick out the *subordinate clauses* from the following sentences and mention of what kind each is:

1. We suggested that Ramen should see a doctor immediately.
2. The match, which was to be played tomorrow, has been postponed.
3. Tell Bimal that he must not be late for the meeting.
4. All the pupils stood up when the teacher entered the classroom.
5. What Lal told us about himself is true.
6. I met the lady who lives next door.
7. The nurse took the medicine to the room where the patient was waiting.
8. Rita has kept the books where you can find them easily.
9. Buddha found people suffering and unhappy everywhere he went.
10. Whatever the king ordered had to be done immediately.
11. Examinations are usually held before the school closes for the summer vacation.
12. The song that Sharmila sang was liked by all.
13. Can you tell me where I can find a bookshop?
14. As soon as I get a letter from him, I will tell you.
15. I would like to go home as soon as the rain stops.

Prepositions

Kinds of Prepositions

There are two kinds of prepositions:

1. A preposition, which consists of only one word, is known as a **simple preposition**.
2. A preposition, which is made up of more than one word, is known as a **complex preposition**.

Given below is a list of commonly used *simple* and *complex prepositions*. However, you must always remember that some of these words may also be used as adverbs and/or conjunctions. Whether a word is an adverb, a conjunction or a preposition depends on the work it does in a phrase, a clause or a sentence.

Simple Prepositions			
across	between	near	regarding
after	by	next	round
against	down	of	than
along	during	off	through
amid	except	on	till
among	following	onto	to
around	in	out	until
before	inside	outside	upon
below	into	over	with
beside	like	past	without

Complex Prepositions

along with	for fear of	in front of	in the hope of
as a result of	for the sake of	in keeping with	in view of
as to	in accordance with	in place of	on account of
at the top of	in case of	with reference to	on behalf of
away from	in comparison to	in regard to	out of
by means of	in comparison with	in respect of	owing to
by way of	in consequence of	in sight of	rather than
close to	in contrast to	in spite of	so far as
due to	in course of	in the case of	such as
except for	in favour of	in the face of	together with

Placing of Prepositions

1. A preposition is usually placed before a noun or pronoun:

   (a) I was looking **for** this <u>book</u>. (**book**: noun)

   (b) Ratna was speaking **to** <u>me</u>. (**me**: pronoun)

   In some sentences, we can place the preposition in a different position:

   (c) This is the <u>book</u> I was looking **for**.

2. Sometimes, however, if we change the position of a preposition, the form of a pronoun changes:

   (d) **To** <u>whom</u> were you talking? but <u>Who</u> were you talking **to**?

   The pronoun **whom** has become **who**.

3. Sometimes, if we change the position of a preposition, a pronoun has to be omitted:

   (e) The boys **with** <u>whom</u> I was playing are all close friends. (**whom**: pronoun)

   (f) The boys I was playing **with** are all close friends. (**whom** omitted)

   (g) The house **in** <u>which</u> he lives is very big. (**which**: pronoun)

   (h) The house he lives **in** is very big. (**which** omitted)

Omission of Prepositions

Look at the two pairs of sentences given below:

(a) He <u>gave</u> the pen **to** <u>Ram</u>.   (b) He <u>gave</u> <u>Ram</u> the pen.

(c) Bina's mother <u>bought</u> a dress **for** <u>Bina</u>.

(d) Bina's mother <u>bought</u> <u>Bina</u> a dress.

Note that when we place the <u>indirect object</u> (**Ram**) <u>immediately after the</u> <u>verb</u> (**gave**), <u>the preposition</u> (**to**) <u>is omitted</u>.

Similarly, when the indirect object **Bina** comes immediately after the verb **bought**, the preposition *for* is omitted.

A. Fill in the blanks with *appropriate prepositions*. The number of blanks indicates how many words the preposition that is needed is made up of. You may consult the lists given on pages 59 and 60.

1. The traveller found himself standing .... a lake and a forest.

2. Newton was sitting .... an apple tree.

3. Ram, ... his brother, came to our house yesterday.

4. Rita looked .... the window and saw Rinky standing outside.

5. The thief jumped .... the wall and escaped.

6. A pronoun is used .... a noun.

7. John parked his car .... my house.

8. Shyam tossed the book carelessly .... the table.

9. Just .... the man's head was a light, but I could not see his face.

10. Gopalan put the letter .... the envelope and sealed it.

11. Peter was shouting .... his voice, but nobody could hear him.

12. .... his best efforts, he could not get a ticket for the Test Match.

13. Ali stood .... the stage, so that he could hear the speakers clearly.

14. I looked .... Kalyan, but he turned his face away.

15. The glass fell .... Rinky's hand and broke .... many pieces.

16. Ma poured some milk .... a glass and gave it .... Piku to drink.

17. Roop has been selected to play .... the school football team.

18. Chandni usually goes to school .... bus.

19. We waited .... him till evening.

20. The teacher was angry .... Saurav, for he had not done his work.

B. Rewrite the following sentences, changing the positions of the underlined *prepositions* or omitting them wherever possible:

1. To whom have you given the tickets?
2. I told you to give the tickets to Jayant.
3. From whom have you heard such a strange story?
4. Can you find a good music teacher for me?
5. Mahua bought a present for Sharmila on her birthday.
6. The man for whom you are looking is hiding in that room.
7. From where has Deepa bought all this furniture?
8. When Jayant shifted from Delhi, he gave a lot of furniture to Bishnu.
9. Will you pass the salt to me, please?
10. Sujit sang a song for us.
11. The pupils have always shown the greatest respect for that teacher.
12. The man to whom I was talking is a famous writer.
13. Vikram forgot to give my message to Aditya.
14. The village from where Sonu comes is in Bihar.
15. A man falls in love with the place he has lived in all his life.
16. The messenger brought some good news for the king.
17. The people with whom Rajesh was dealing were all dishonest.
18. To whom has the task been given?
19. Sanjit sent some money to his mother.
20. If you come here, I shall show something interesting to you.

Active and Passive Voice

14

Look at the following two sentences carefully:

(a) My dog **chased** the black cat.

(b) The black cat **was chased** by my dog.

The two sentences say the same thing but in different ways. The first sentence tells us what our <u>dog did</u>; the second tells us what <u>was done to the black cat</u>.

If we analyse the sentences further, we find that:

1. In (a), **chased** is the <u>verb</u> and **dog** is its <u>subject</u>.

   [Q: Who/What chased a cat?   Ans: (The) dog]

   Secondly, **cat** is the <u>object</u> of the verb **chased**.

   [Q: Chased what/whom?   Ans: (a black) cat]

   So, in (a), it is the **subject** that is the <u>doer</u> or <u>performer</u> of the action — **chased**. In other words, the **subject** is the **agent**.

   Since what the subject <u>did</u> affected the object, **cat**, the verb **chased** is transitive.

   But, in (b), the <u>verb</u> is **was chased** and the <u>subject</u> is **cat**.

   [Who/What was chased?   Ans: (The black) cat]

   In this sentence, the **subject** is not the **agent**, because the subject did not do anything. On the contrary, something <u>was done to the subject</u>. It is the subject which was acted upon, or was at the receiving end of the action.

   Secondly, as the subject did not do anything, the question of somebody or something else being affected by the action of the subject does not arise. So, the verb **was chased** does not have an <u>object</u>. It is intransitive.

   A sentence, in which the subject of the verb is the <u>agent</u> or doer of the action denoted by the verb, is said to be in the *active voice*.

   [**active** = energetic; working]

A sentence in which the subject does not perform the action denoted by the verb but is acted upon is said to be in the **passive voice**.

[**passive** = not active; acted upon]

If you look at the two verbs, you will find that they are different forms of the same verb: **chased**, **was chased**. So, the **form** of a verb tells us its *voice*.

We can, therefore, say that **voice** is that form of a verb which shows whether or not the subject of the verb is the <u>agent</u> of the action denoted by the verb.

Differences between Active and Passive

We can now summarize the differences between the ***active voice*** and the ***passive voice***:

1. The subject of an *active verb* is the agent of the action denoted by the verb.
2. The subject of a *passive verb* is not the agent of the action denoted by the verb. It is acted upon or is affected by the action denoted by the verb. It is passive, that is, inactive.
3. In a sentence in the *passive voice*, the agent of the action denoted by the verb may or may not be mentioned.
4. In a sentence in the *passive voice*, if we want to mention the <u>agent</u>, we have to use a <u>preposition</u> after the *passive verb*, and then mention the agent. The agent then becomes the <u>object of the preposition</u> used:

    (a) The black cat <u>was chased</u> **by** our dog.

    (b) The room <u>was filled</u> **with** smoke.

In (a), the <u>preposition</u> **by** is used after the passive verb **was chased**, and then the <u>agent</u> **dog** is mentioned. The agent (noun) **dog** becomes the object of **by**.

In (b), the <u>preposition</u> **with** is used after the passive verb **was filled**. The <u>agent</u> **smoke** is then mentioned. The agent (noun) **smoke** becomes the object of **with**.

5. The **form** of the *passive verb* is different from that of the corresponding *active verb*.

   Usually, the *passive verb* is made up of an appropriate form of the verb **be** + the **past participle** form of the active verb, like ***was chased***, ***was filled***.

   However, when the agent is not mentioned, an appropriate form of the verb **get** is sometimes used instead of **be** with the past participle:

   (i) Many soldiers **got** <u>killed</u> in that battle.

   [past tense of **get** + past participle of the verb <u>kill</u>]

   (ii) The children **got** <u>lost</u> in the crowd at the fair.

   [past tense of **get** + past participle of the verb <u>lose</u>]

   (iii) Ram will surely **get** elected President this time.

   [present tense of **get** + past participle of the verb <u>elect</u>]

A. Say which of the following sentences are in the *active* and which in the *passive voice*:

1. Tom was reading a storybook.
2. This story has been written by a famous writer.
3. The boy easily swam across to the other side of the lake.
4. The English channel has been crossed many times.
5. Galileo did not invent the telescope.
6. The telescope was probably invented by a medieval Arab scientist.
7. Nobody should talk in a library.
8. Please tell me your name.
9. Tea and coffee will be served at 11 a.m.
10. We do not like this hotel at all.
11. This book has been chewed up by my dog.
12. All the food was finished within an hour.

13. The treaty was signed by all the nations.
14. Julius Caesar was killed by the conspirators.
15. Brutus killed Caesar because of his love for Rome.

Changing from Active to Passive

It is now clear that in changing the voice from *active* to *passive*, we have to make certain changes. They are summarized below:

1. The object of the active verb becomes the subject of the passive verb.
    It, therefore, follows that usually only active transitive verbs which can have objects can be changed into passive.
    So, all sentences in the active voice cannot be changed into the passive.

2. The subject of the active verb or the agent can be mentioned only with the help of a preposition: usually **by** or **with**.
    The passive verb is followed by the preposition **by** or **with**, and then the <u>agent</u> is mentioned. The <u>agent</u>, therefore, becomes the <u>object</u> of the preposition used.

3. An *active transitive verb* may have two objects: <u>direct</u> and <u>indirect</u>.
    (a) Sita gave Veena a book.
    [Q: Sita gave what/whom?   Ans: (a) book   Ans: Veena]
    So, **book** is the <u>direct object</u>, and **Veena** the <u>indirect object</u>.
    In changing the voice to passive, any one of the objects can be made the subject of the passive verb. The other object may be retained as the object of the passive verb, and is then known as the ***retained object***.
    (b) **Veena** was given a **book** by Sita.
    (c) A **book** was given to **Veena** by Sita.

    In (b), **book** which was the direct object of the active verb becomes the ***retained object***.

    In (c), **Veena** which was the indirect object of the active verb becomes the ***retained object***.

    Note, however, that in a sentence like (c), we usually use the preposition **to** before the retained object:

(d) A **book** was given **to** <u>Veena</u> by Sita.

Veena would then become an object of the preposition **to**.

Here is another example:

(e) Mr Sinha taught us mathematics.   *Active Voice*

(f) We were taught mathematics by Mr Sinha.   *Passive Voice*

(g) Mathematics was taught us by Mr Sinha.   *Passive Voice*

In (f), **mathematics** (direct object in active voice) is the ***retained object***.

In (g), **us** (indirect object in active voice) is the ***retained object***.

4. Depending upon the tense of the active verb, an appropriate passive form of the verb **be** has to be used with the **past participle** of the active verb to get the passive form.

(i) Active: A thief **stole** my watch.

Passive: My watch **was stolen** by a thief.

[The tense of the active verb is <u>simple past</u>.

So, the appropriate passive form of the verb <u>be</u> to be used here is **was**.

The past participle form of the active verb <u>steal</u> is **stolen**.]

(ii) Active: I **have done** my work.

Passive: My work **has been done** by me.

[The tense of the active verb is <u>present perfect</u>.

So, the appropriate passive form of the verb <u>be</u> to be used here is **has been**.

The past participle form of the verb <u>do</u> is **done**.]

(iii) Active: The children **were singing** a song.

Passive: A song **was being sung** by the children.

[The tense of the active verb is <u>past continuous</u>. So, the appropriate passive form of the verb <u>be</u> to be used is **was being**.

The past participle form of the verb <u>sing</u> is <u>sung</u>.]

Given on the next page is a table which gives a summary of the active and passive forms of the verb **do** in the various tenses.

Tense	Active	Passive
simple present	He <u>does</u> it.	It <u>is done</u> by him.
present continuous	He <u>is doing</u> it.	It <u>is being done</u> by him.
present perfect	He <u>has done</u> it.	It <u>has been done</u> by him.
simple past	He <u>did</u> it.	It <u>was done</u> by him.
past continuous	He <u>was doing</u> it.	It <u>was being done</u> by him.
past perfect	He <u>had done</u> it.	It <u>had been done</u> by him.
simple future	He <u>will do</u> it.	It <u>will be done</u> by him.
future continuous	He <u>will be doing</u> it.	It <u>will be being done</u> by him. (rarely used)
future perfect	He <u>will have done</u> it.	It <u>will have been done</u> by him.

5. When an active transitive verb of incomplete predication is made passive, the objective complement becomes a subjective complement, because the object of the active verb becomes the subject of the passive verb.

   (i) Active: The members elected <u>Hari</u> **President**.

                  Hari − object; President − objective complement

       Passive: *<u>Hari</u> was elected* **President** *by the members.*

                  Hari − subject; President − subjective complement

   (ii) Active: Everybody called <u>Tim</u> **a fool**.

                  Tim − object; a fool − objective complement

       Passive: *<u>Tim</u> was called* **a fool** *by everybody.*

                  Tim − subject; a fool − subjective complement

Given below are two examples of how an ***imperative sentence*** may be changed from the active to the passive voice.

   (i) Active: Close the door.

       Passive: Let the door be closed.

   (ii) Active: Please switch off your cell phones during the show.

       Passive: Cell phones should be switched off during the show.

Some General Observations

1. The term **voice** is applicable to verbs, clauses and sentences.

2. There are two voices: the *active* and the *passive*. The *active voice* is the basic type.

3. The two voices enable us to look at the same action in two different ways. The active voice looks at the action from the point of view of the agent; the passive voice looks at the action from the point of view of the person or object affected by the action.

4. The passive voice is generally used in writing reports, describing scientific experiments, etc., for in such cases what is done, has been done or needs to be done is more important than the agent.

B. Change the *voice*:

1. The dinner was cooked by Shyam.
2. Ring the bell.
3. You have to perform these experiments.
4. Rules must be obeyed.
5. He was surprised by the news.
6. The dishes were washed by us.
7. The sight enchanted us.
8. The Ganga is worshipped as a goddess by most Indians.
9. Who wrote the *Mahabharata*?
10. The horse was led to its stable by the groom.
11. V. Anand won the match.
12. Clean this table properly.
13. Sita kept all her money in the bank.
14. I could not remember his name.
15. Geetha sang a very sad song.

Direct and Indirect Speech–1

Recapitulation

Direct speech is one way of reporting what somebody has said.

    (a) Rinky said, *'I have a brother called Piku.'*

    (b) Chandni asked Rinky, *'Which school does he go to?'*

    (c) Rinky replied, *'He is in a boarding school.'*

    (d) Chandni exclaimed, *'How exciting!'*

1.   All the above sentences are in ***direct speech***, because what the speakers – Rinky and Chandni – said are reported word for word.

2.   Since direct speech quotes the actual words used by a speaker, what the speaker said is put within quotation marks and is known as the ***quote***.

    [In the above sentences the ***quotes*** are printed in *italics*.]

    When you use quotation marks, you have to be particularly careful about the use of other punctuation marks. This has been dealt with in Book 3. Note also that nowadays a single quotation mark is usually used ('.....') instead of a double (".....").

3.   A sentence in direct speech consists of two parts:

    (a) Rinky **said**,   + 'I have a brother called Piku.'

    (b) Chandni **asked** Rinky,   + 'Which school does he go to?'

    (c) Rinky **replied**,   + 'He is in a boarding school.'

    (d) Chandni **exclaimed**,   + 'How exciting!'

    (i) The verbs – *said, asked, replied, exclaimed* – are called ***verbs of speaking*** or ***reporting verbs***.

   (ii) The first part that contains the *reporting verb* is known as the ***reporting clause***, for it has a subject and a predicate:

    (a) Q: *Who* said?   Ans: Rinky (subject) + predicate: said, '.....'

    (b) Q: *Who* asked?   Ans: Chandni (subject) + predicate: asked, '.....'

(c) Q: *Who* replied? Ans: Rinky (subject) + predicate: replied, '.....'

(d) Q: *Who* exclaimed? Ans: Chandni (subject) + predicate: exclaimed, '.....'

(iii) In direct speech, a *reporting verb* is the **main verb**, and the *quote* is the **direct object** of the main verb.

Rinky said *what*? Chandni asked *what*?

Rinky replied *what*? Chandni exclaimed *what*?

In each case the *quote* answers the question.

(iv) The **reporting** or **main verb** may also have an **indirect object**:

(b) Q: Chandni asked *whom*? Ans: Rinky (indirect object)

Q: Chandni asked *what*? Ans: quote (direct object)

4. In direct speech, the *quote* may come at the beginning or at the end of a sentence.

(a) *'I have a brother called Piku,'* <u>said</u> Rinky.

(b) *'Which school does he go to?'* Chandni <u>asked</u> Rinky.

(c) *'He is in a boarding school,'* <u>replied</u> Rinky.

(d) *'How exciting!'* <u>exclaimed</u> Chandni.

Note that when the *quote* comes at the beginning, the reporting verb usually comes before its subject. But if the subject is a pronoun, the reporting verb is usually placed after its subject.

(e) *'I have a brother called Piku,'* she <u>said</u>.

(f) *'Which school does he go to?'* he <u>asked</u>.

A. Pick out the *reporting verb* from each sentence, and separate the *reporting clause* from the *quote*:

1. I asked Jeff, 'Have you met John?'
2. Piku said, 'I like music.'
3. Roop told his mother, 'I don't want to go to school.'
4. The doctor insisted, 'You must take this medicine.'
5. The boy asked me, 'What is the time?'
6. I replied, 'It is five o'clock.'

7. He cried, 'I shall be late for the cricket match!'

8. Deep's father told him, 'Don't play in the rain.'

9. Jayant invited Gurmeet, 'Come and have a cup of tea.'

10. Zafar said, 'Thank you.'

B. Rewrite the following sentences, using a *quotation mark* wherever required:

1. I told him, Do not disturb the class.

2. His mother said, John is sleeping.

3. My friend pleaded, Let us not quarrel.

4. The teacher asked, Why do you always get your sums wrong?

5. Chandni screamed, There is a cockroach under the table!

6. The doctor asked, Are you feeling very weak?

7. All the supporters roared, Goal!

8. Mahua told her mother, Please give me a glass of water.

9. He said, Please forgive me for what I have done.

10. Roop replied, I do not know where Rinky has gone.

C. Rewrite the following sentences, transferring the *quote* from the end of each sentence to its beginning:

1. Rashid inquired, 'Have you met my brother?'

2. The mother whispered to the child, 'Sleep, my baby.'

3. The policeman asked, 'Has anybody seen anything suspicious?'

4. He said, 'Father, please let me go and watch the match!'

5. The teacher said, 'Well done, Hari! You have got the highest marks in English.'

D. Rewrite the following sentences, transferring the *quote* from the beginning to the end of each sentence:

1. 'Do not go near the lake,' the guard warned the children.

2. 'Do you take sugar with your tea?' asked the lady.

3. 'India is sure to win this match,' remarked the commentator.

4. 'The patient is doing well,' observed the doctor.

5. 'Let us go for a walk,' suggested Ram.

Use of 'Said' and 'Told'

Two of the most frequently used reporting verbs are **said** and **told**. There is, however, a difference in the way they are used.

   (a) Ram **told** <u>me</u>, 'I am going home.'

   (b) Ram **said** *to* <u>me</u>, 'I am going home.'

Told usually takes two objects: a direct object and an indirect one.

Here, <u>me</u> is the indirect object and the <u>quote</u> is the direct object.

Said takes only one object: a direct one – the <u>quote</u>.

So, we use **said** when we just want to report what somebody said and do not want to add anything further.

If we want to use **said** and want to mention to whom something has been said, we have to use the preposition **to** after **said**.

Correct: I told him, 'Don't shout like that.'

Incorrect: I told <u>to</u> him, 'Don't shout like that.'

               (**to** is not used with **told** in this way)

Correct: Shyam said to Ram, 'Give me a pen, please.'

Incorrect: Shyam said Ram, 'Give me a pen, please.'

               (**to** must be used after **said**)

E. Rewrite the following sentences, filling in the blanks with *reporting verbs* chosen from those given within brackets, and using a *quotation mark* wherever required:

1. May I come in? .... the visitor. *(asked, replied)*

2. Aparna ...., I don't like drinking milk. *(asked, said)*

3. Nishat .... his mother, I have lost my pen. *(replied, told, asked)*

4. Don't get lost, ... the mother to her child. *(told, said)*

5. The teacher .... Ravi, Do your work quietly. *(said, asked, told)*

6. Jayant ...., Hurrah! My vacation starts tomorrow.
   (asked, exclaimed)

7. I ...., Ma, I am going out. *(told, said, asked)*

8. Mahua .... Sharmila, I shall see you tomorrow. *(said, asked, told)*

9. Can you point out Nepal on the map of the world? .... the teacher. *(told, asked)*

Indirect Speech

Indirect speech is another way of reporting what somebody has said. In indirect speech, we do not use exactly the same words used by the speaker. Given below are five pairs of sentences. Study them carefully.

1. *Direct speech* : 'Where are you going?' asked Sita.

   Indirect speech : Sita asked (me) where I was going.

2. *Direct speech* : Hari said, 'I shall meet you tomorrow.'

   Indirect speech : Hari said that he would meet me the next day.

3. *Direct speech* : Gopal told John, 'Be careful.'

   Indirect speech : Gopal advised John to be careful.

4. *Direct speech* : They exclaimed, 'What a beautiful picture!'

   Indirect speech : They said that it was a very beautiful picture.

F. Copy the sentences of Group I in your exercise book. Then below each sentence write the sentence from Group II that matches it.

Group I

1. The Pobble exclaimed, 'I have lost my toes!'

2. Many years ago, Galileo had declared, 'The earth goes round the sun.'

3. Sita told me, 'Be very careful when you cross this busy street.'

4. 'Will you please pass me the jug of water?' said John.

5. Ram said, 'Come, let us play a new game.'

6. 'You will be a famous man one day,' said the astrologer.

7. Shyam said, 'How hot it is today!'

8. The messenger said, 'Alas! the king is dead.'

9. 'I am the cleverest boy in this class,' said Gopal.

10. 'Why are you sitting here all alone?' Mahua asked Sharmila.

Group II

1. Ram suggested that we should play a new game.
2. Gopal boasted that he was the cleverest boy in that class.
3. Many years ago, Galileo had declared that the earth goes round the sun.
4. John requested me to pass him the jug of water.
5. Shyam exclaimed that it was very hot that day.
6. The Pobble exclaimed sadly that he had lost his toes.
7. The messenger declared mournfully that the king was dead.
8. Sita warned me to be very careful when crossing that busy street.
9. Mahua asked Sharmila why she was sitting there all alone.
10. The astrologer prophesied that I would be a famous man one day.

The Report

In indirect speech, what the speaker said is called the *report*.

As in the case of direct speech, we can divide a sentence containing indirect speech into two parts:

1. The **reporting** or **main clause** that contains the **reporting verb**.
2. The **report**.

Note that like the **quote** in direct speech, the **report** in indirect speech is the **object** of the **reporting verb**. If the reporting verb has two objects, the **report** is the **direct object**.

(a) Ram **told** <u>me</u> <u>to give him a pen</u>.

Q: Ram told whom?   Ans: me (indirect object)

Q: Ram told what?   Ans: report (direct object)

G. Pick out the *reporting verb* from each sentence, and separate the *reporting* or *main clause* of the sentence from the *report*:

1. He said that he had come to Kolkata by train.
2. The teacher told the class that Wednesday would be a holiday.
3. The doctor asked the patient what medicine he had taken.
4. The general ordered the soldiers to retreat.
5. Sita requested Veena to lend her a book.

Direct and Indirect Speech–2

16

As you know, what somebody has said can be reported either in **_direct speech_** or in **_indirect speech_**. There are, however, some important differences between them. So, if we are asked to change direct speech into indirect, or indirect into direct, that is, to change the **mode of narration**, we have to make some changes in the given sentence or sentences. Some of the more important changes are discussed below.

Changing the Mode of Narration

1. The first thing that we must remember is that the changes that have to be made in turning direct speech into indirect, or indirect into direct, depend on various things, like:

    (i) who is speaking to whom, and

    (ii) the manner or the way in which the speaker is speaking: is the speaker simply stating something, or giving an order, or making a request, etc.?

    In other words, we must not only make sure that the **meaning** of the sentence **does not change**, but also that we capture the **mood** of the speaker: we must try and indicate whether the speaker is angry, or sad, or excited, or full of joy, and so on.

2. Let us begin by comparing direct speech with indirect:

    Direct : He told his mother, 'I am hungry.'

    Indirect : He told his mother that he was hungry.

    You will notice that in the change from direct to indirect speech:

    (i) Quotation marks have been omitted.

    (ii) The reporting verb has not changed in any way.

    (iii) The preposition **_that_** has been <u>added after</u> the reporting verb.

    (iv) The reporting clause has not changed in any way.

    (v) The **_report_** is different from the **_quote_**.

So, the main **changes** have taken place **in** the **report** or that part of the sentence that contains <u>what has been said or spoken.</u>

These changes are:

(i) The pronoun **I** (first person) has become **he** (third person).

(ii) The verb **am** (present tense) has become **was** (past tense).

You should, therefore, remember:

(i) In indirect speech, **that** is usually added after the reporting verb, like **said**, **told**, **whispered**, etc. This **that** may be omitted, particularly in spoken or colloquial English.

Direct : Babloo told Raman, 'It is raining.'

Indirect : Babloo told Raman **that** it was raining.

or

Babloo told Raman it was raining.

(ii) If there is a pronoun in the **quote**, it may be necessary to change the **person of the pronoun** in the **report** to make the meaning of the report clear.

In the following example, **I** becomes **he** to make it clear that Ram was speaking about himself.

Direct : Ram said, 'Ma, **I** am feeling ill.'

Indirect : Ram told his mother that **he** was feeling ill.

If this change is not made, the sentence will read:

Ram told his mother that I was feeling ill.

This would mean that it was not Ram but the speaker, who is reporting what Ram had said, had been feeling ill.

If there is more than one personal pronoun in the **quote**, it may be necessary to change some or all of them in the **report** to make the meaning of what has been said clear. It might also be necessary to replace a personal pronoun with the noun it stands for:

Direct : Ramen asked Ram, 'Are **you** my brother's friend?'

Indirect : Ramen asked Ram whether **Ram** was his brother's friend.

Note that if the pronoun that has to be changed is the **subject** of a verb, that is, if the subject-pronoun is replaced with a pronoun of a different person or a noun, the **verb** must also be changed, if necessary, to agree with its new **subject** in number and person.

In the quote *Are you my brother's friend*, *you* is the **subject** of the verb *are*.

In the report, *you* (second person) changes to *Ram* (third person). So the verb *are* (plural) also changes to *was* (singular) to agree with its new **subject** Ram in **person** and **number**.

(iii) If the reporting verb is not in the *present* or *future* tense, the **tense** of the verb in the **report** changes from what it was in the **quote**:

Direct : John **told** Mary, 'I am going to school.'

Indirect: John **told** Mary that he was going to school.

Since the tense of the reporting verb *told* is the simple *past*, the tense of the verb in the report has to be changed from the *present continuous* to the *past continuous*, from *am going* to *was going*. Another example of this change is given below:

Direct : Jeet **said**, 'I shall be meeting Hari tomorrow.'

Indirect: Jeet **said** that he would be meeting Hari the next day.

A. Given below are pairs of sentences—the first is in *direct speech*, the second is the same sentence in *indirect speech*. Fill in the blanks in each second sentence with *appropriate words*. Two examples have been given below to help you.

(a) *Direct* : He said, 'I am tired.'

   Indirect : He said .... he .... tired.

   Answer : He said <u>that</u> he <u>was</u> tired.

(b) *Direct* : His mother told him, 'I am going to the market.'

   Indirect : His mother .... him that .... going to the market.

   Answer : His mother <u>told</u> him that <u>she</u> <u>was</u> going to the market.

1. *Direct:* He told me, 'You are no longer my friend.'

   Indirect: He .... me that .... no longer .... friend.

2. *Direct:* 'Why are you crying?' Alice asked Mary.

   Indirect: Alice .... Mary .... she ....

3. *Direct:* My father warned me, 'Don't eat too many chocolates.'

   Indirect: My father .... me not to .... too many chocolates.

4. The teacher told John, 'Read the poem carefully.'

   The teacher told John that .... should .... the poem carefully.

5. Rinky told Piku, 'You are being very naughty.'

   Rinky .... Piku that .... being very naughty.

6. 'May I borrow your pen?' Rajesh asked Gopalan.

   Rajesh .... whether .... borrow .... pen.

7. 'Please sit down,' Mr Roy told the visitor.

   Mr Roy requested the visitor .... down.

8. The doctor told Jane, 'You must drink a cup of milk every day.'

   The doctor told Jane that .... a cup of milk every day.

9. His mother asked John, 'Have you washed your hands?'

   His mother .... John if he .... washed .... hands.

10. 'Who in this class knows this poem by heart?' asked the teacher.

    The teacher asked .... in that .... poem by heart.

11. Raja groaned, 'I think I have broken my leg.'

    Groaning, Raja .... that he .... that .... had .... his leg.

12. Mary confessed, 'I am the one who has broken the glass.'

    Mary .... that .... was the one who .... broken the glass.

13. The Giant roared, 'Who has dared to enter my garden?'

The Giant .... and .... who .... to enter his garden.

14. 'Read the question paper carefully,' the teacher advised him.

The teacher .... him to .... the question paper ....

15. Deep muttered to himself, 'I am a fool.'

Deep .... to himself that .... a fool.

16. The visitor remarked, 'Your dog is very friendly.'

The visitor remarked .... dog .... very friendly.

17. The boy asked, 'May I sit down and rest for a while?'

The boy asked .... he could .... down and .... for a while.

18. Mahua told Sharmila, 'Do not buy any flowers.'

Mahua .... Sharmila not .... any flowers.

19. Roop boasted, 'I can easily swim across this river.'

Roop boasted .... he .... easily .... across .... river.

20. The Queen told Alice, 'Keep quiet.'

The Queen .... Alice to .... quiet.

B. Here is a set of similar exercises, but the second sentence of each pair is in *direct speech*. Fill in the blanks, inserting *quotation marks* wherever required:

1. *Indirect:* I told him that he was sure to get elected captain of the team.

Direct: I told him, ... sure to get elected captain of the team.

2. *Indirect:* I asked him why he was not going to school.

Direct: I .... him, Why .... you not going to school?

3. *Indirect:* My father told me to go and fetch the newspaper.

Direct: My father told .... , Go and .... the newspaper.

4. John requested Jeff to lend him a pen.

John said, Jeff, please .... a pen.

5. Shyam told me that he had been ill.

   Shyam .... me, ... been ill.

6. His teacher advised him never to lose his temper.

   His teacher told him, Never lose .... temper.

7. Ravi asked Piku why he was looking so sad.

   Ravi .... Piku, Why are .... looking so sad?

8. Piku replied that he was sad, because India had lost the match.

   Piku replied, ... sad, because India .... lost the match.

9. Tom asked his father whether he could go and see the play.

   Father, may .... go and .... the play? .... Tom.

10. Ramen said that his brother had fallen down and broken his arm.

    Ramen said, ... brother .... fallen down and broken .... arm.

11. Ram whispered to his brother to keep quiet or he would wake their mother up.

    Ram .... to his brother, ... quiet or .... wake mother up.

12. Jayant suggested that he and we should stop quarrelling.

    Jayant ...., Let .... stop quarrelling.

13. The mechanic enquired what was wrong with his television set.

    The mechanic ...., What .... wrong with .... television set?

14. Everybody said that it was a very silly mistake.

    What a ....! .... everybody.

15. The child asked her mother to buy her a doll.

    The child ...., Ma, please .... a doll.

The **speaking** or **reporting verbs** in all the sentences of **Ex. B** are in the **past tense**. Now let us look at some sentences in which the reporting verbs are in some form of the **present** or **future tense**.

(a) *Direct* : My father always **says**, 'Getting up early in the morning <u>is</u> a good habit.'

Indirect : My father always **says** that getting up early in the morning <u>is</u> a good habit.

(b) *Direct* : Ram **has told** me, '<u>I am going</u> to Delhi during the summer vacation.'

Indirect : Ram **has told** me that <u>he is going</u> to Delhi during the summer vacation.

(c) *Direct* : When my father sees my Report Card, he **will say**, 'I <u>am</u> proud of you.'

Indirect : When my father sees my Report Card, he **will say** that he <u>is</u> proud of me.

(d) *Direct* : Jayant **has told** them, 'I <u>did</u> not <u>go</u> to Ramen's house today.'

Indirect : Jayant **has told** them that he <u>did</u> not <u>go</u> to Ramen's house that day.

We can, therefore, say that when the reporting verb is in some form of the present or future tense, in changing direct speech to indirect:

1. The **tense** of the verb in the **report** (i.e. indirect speech) does not change from what it is in the **quote** (i.e. direct speech).

2. The **personal pronouns** in the **quote** may have to be **changed** in the **report**. See examples (b), (c), (d).

3. If we change the **person** of a personal pronoun, which is the **subject** of a verb, that verb must agree with its new pronoun–subject in number and person.

Direct : Ram always says, '**I** <u>am</u> more intelligent than Hari.'

Indirect : Ram always says that **he** <u>is</u> more intelligent than Hari.

The person of the subject–pronoun has changed from the first to the third person. The verb **am**, which agreed with its subject **I** in number and person, has to be changed to **is** to agree with its new subject **he** in number and person.

C. Change the *mode of narration*:

1. Whenever Chandan sees me, he asks, 'How are you?'
2. He still says, 'I am innocent.'
3. When John hears this, he will say, 'You are a fool.'
4. He always complains, 'The roads of Kolkata are never repaired.'
5. Ram has repeatedly told me, 'Nepal is a beautiful country.'
6. I shall certainly tell Ram, 'You have done the right thing.'
7. 'Why are you always late?' his teacher asks him every day.
8. Jeff never says, 'I am sorry, for I have done something wrong.'
9. The manager of the hotel has told me, 'You can stay as long as you like.'
10. Every morning, after getting up from bed, he says, 'I am tired.'
11. When I get home, I shall tell Ma, 'I shall always do what you say.'
12. The proverb says, 'Health is better than wealth.'
13. My father will ask me, 'Why have you come home so late?'
14. Rita has told me, 'I do not like Raja at all.'
15. Everybody says, 'David will become a champion tennis player one day.'

Changes: A Summary

Verbs

1. If the tense of the reporting verb is some form of the present or future, the tense of the verb in the report remains the same as that in the quote.
2. If the tense of the reporting verb is some form of the past, the tense of the verb in the report has to be changed in most cases:

Guidelines:

simple present changes to *simple past*

present continuous changes to *past continuous*

present perfect changes to *past perfect*

simple past changes to *past perfect* or *does not change*

past continuous does not change

past perfect does not change

'can', ' will', 'shall', 'may' change to *'could', 'would', 'should', 'might'*

'could', 'would', 'should', 'might' do not change

'must' does not change or changes to *'had to'*

3. If the report says something that is still true, the tense of the verb in the report does not change from what it is in the quote even if the reporting verb is in the past tense.

Direct : Our teacher <u>said</u>, 'The earth **goes** round the sun.'

Indirect: Our teacher <u>said</u> that the earth **goes** round the sun.

Pronouns

Often, personal pronouns have to be changed to avoid confusion. The changes depend on who is saying what. It may sometimes even be necessary, as we have seen, to replace a pronoun with a noun to make what the speaker said clear.

Direct : Ram told the police, '**He** came in through the door at the back.'

Indirect : Ram told the police that the **thief** came in through the door at the back.

If we say, 'Ram told the police that *he* came in through the door at the back,' it would mean that Ram himself came in through the door at the back.

Adjectives and Adverbs

These may have to be changed. The changes which are usually necessary are listed below:

Direct Speech	Indirect Speech
this	that/the
these	those/the
here	there
now	then
today	that day
tonight	that night
tomorrow	the next day/the following day
the day after tomorrow	in two days' time

yesterday	the day before
the day before yesterday	two days before/two days ago
next week/year	the following week/year
this week	that week
last week	the week before
next Monday	the following Monday

Questions

1. You must have noticed that in changing direct questions into indirect, we have to change the interrogative sentence into a statement. The question mark is, therefore, omitted.

   Direct : He **said**, 'Where does Ram live?'

   Indirect : He **asked** where Ram lived.

2. If the reporting verb is *say*, we have to change it into a verb of inquiry, like **asked**, **inquired**, **wanted to know**, etc.

3. If the direct question begins with a word like **how**, **who**, **when**, **where**, **why**, that word has to be repeated in the indirect question:

   Direct : He <u>said</u>, '**When** is Shiva going home?'

   Indirect : He <u>asked</u> **when** Shiva was going home.

4. Sometimes, the word *if* or *whether* has to be used in the indirect question:

   Direct : He asked, 'Does Ram live here?'

   Indirect : He asked <u>if/whether</u> Ram lived there.

Exclamations, Commands, Requests, Advice

In changing an exclamatory or imperative sentence into indirect, we have to use a suitable reporting verb to suggest as clearly as possible the nature of what was said: was it a command, a request, an appeal, or an exclamation, etc? Depending on who said what in what way, any of the following may be chosen as a reporting verb:

exclaim, command, beg, entreat, request, pray, bless, advise, implore, ask, order, invite, request, urge, warn, recommend, insist, remind, forbid

Direct : Kiran told Suman, 'Come and have dinner with me.'

Indirect: Kiran invited Suman to go and have dinner with him.

Direct : 'Go and help the poor villagers,' said the priest.

Indirect: The priest urged (the people) to help the poor villagers.

D. Change the *mode of narration*:

1. Suman said, 'Do you know what time it is?'

2. 'Do not enter without permission,' said the notice on the gate.

3. Jayant told me, 'I am going to Chennai tonight.'

4. Vimal asked Ravi, 'Are you a member of the school football team?'

5. 'Please pass me the salt,' said Mary to John.

6. Geeta said, 'I picked these flowers myself yesterday.'

7. Suneeta inquired, 'Niti, will you be seeing Rita this evening?'

8. Mahua exclaimed, 'Piku, you have cut your hand!'

9. The boys shouted, 'Come out at once! The house is on fire.'

10. The proverb says, 'A rolling stone gathers no moss.'

11. The sentry said, 'Halt! Where are you going?'

12. The villagers told the hunter, 'Save us from the attacks of the man-eating tiger.'

13. 'May I speak to the manager of the bank, please?' said the lady.

14. Jeevan said, 'Govinda will leave for his village tomorrow.'

15. The farmers said, 'Alas! Unless it rains, we shall lose all our crop.'

16. Jayant asked me, 'What are you doing this evening?'

17. His sister told him, 'Please wait for me near the bus stop.'

18. Our book says, 'The earth is not perfectly round.'

19. The little boy went on saying, 'I want to go home.'

20. 'Do not bathe in the sea here,' the coastguard warned us.

21. The old lady told Tom, 'Come here and listen to what I say.'

22. John said, 'Could you lend me this book for a day?'

23. The new captain has told the team, 'We shall certainly win this match.'

24. John said, 'I shall try my best to help you.'

25. 'Let no man tell me that I have not done my duty,' said the soldier.

17

Dorothy and Her Friends

So once more the little company set off upon the journey, the Lion walking with *stately strides* at Dorothy's side. Toto did not approve of this new *comrade* at first, for he could not forget how nearly he had been *crushed* between the Lion's great jaws. But after a time he became more at ease, and *presently* Toto and the Cowardly Lion had grown to be good friends.

During the rest of that day there was no other adventure to spoil the peace of their journey. Once, indeed, the Tin Woodman stepped upon a beetle that was crawling along the road, and killed the poor little thing. This made the poor Woodman very unhappy, for he was always careful not to hurt any living creature; and as he walked along he wept several tears of sorrow and regret. These tears ran slowly down his face and over the *hinges* of his jaw, and there they *rusted*. When Dorothy presently asked him a question, the Tin Woodman could not open his mouth, for his jaws were tightly rusted together. He became greatly frightened at this and made many motions to Dorothy to relieve him, but she could not understand. The Lion was also puzzled. But the Scarecrow *seized* the oilcan from Dorothy's basket and oiled the Woodman's jaws, so that after a few moments he could talk as well as before.

'This will teach me a lesson,' said he, 'to look where I step. For if I should kill another bug or beetle I should surely cry again, and crying rusts my jaws so that I cannot speak.'

After that, he walked very carefully, with his eyes on the road, and when he saw a tiny ant toiling by he would step over it, so as not to harm it. The Tin Woodman knew very well he had no heart, and therefore he took great care never to be cruel or unkind to anything.

'You people with hearts,' he said, 'have something to guide you, and need never do wrong. But I have no heart, and so I must be very careful. When Oz gives me a heart, of course, I needn't mind so much.'

(Adapted from *The Wonderful Wizard of Oz* by L. F. Baum)

A. Read the passage and answer the following questions:

1. Why did Toto not approve of the Lion at first?
2. Why did the Tin Woodman weep?
3. What happened to the Tin Woodman when he wept?
4. Who helped the Woodman and how?
5. What lesson did the Woodman learn from what happened to him, and how did he behave after that?
6. Who would give the Tin Woodman a heart? Do you think he really needed one to be kind?

B. Match each *word* with the *meaning* it has in the passage:

1. stately   (i) grand and dignified
              (ii) to speak fluently
              (iii) cowardly

2. stride   (i) to scatter
              (ii) to walk with long steps
              (iii) to guide

3. comrade   (i) a companion
               (ii) a trickster
               (iii) a fierce animal

4. crushed (i) supported
   (ii) struggled
   (iii) pressed or squeezed very hard
5. presently (i) keeping time
   (ii) soon
   (iii) a gift
6. seized (i) stopped
   (ii) grabbed
   (iii) looked
7. hinges (i) a small piece of metal on which something swings as it opens or closes
   (ii) a person who stops someone else from doing something
   (iii) the rear legs of an animal
8. rust (i) to sound like crushed paper or dry leaves
   (ii) to hurry
   (iii) to become covered with a reddish–brown substance formed by the action of air and water on metal

C. Rewrite the last sentence of the passage expanding the *contraction* it contains to its full form.

D. Which of the underlined groups of words are *phrases* and which *clauses*? Mention of what kind each is.

1. <u>As he walked along</u>, he wept several tears <u>of sorrow</u>.
2. <u>When Dorothy asked him a question</u>, the Tin Woodman could not open his mouth.
3. 'You people <u>with hearts</u>,' he said, 'have something to guide you.'

E. Pick out *five* words formed with *prefixes* and *suffixes* from the following sentences:

1. This made the poor Woodman very unhappy.
2. These tears ran slowly down his face.

3. Crying rusts my jaws.

4. I must be very careful.

F. Fill in the blanks with *appropriate prepositions* taken from the passage:

1. My father does not approve .... my habit of reading in bed.

2. The thief snatched the bag .... her hands and ran away.

3. The old man walked .... unsteady steps to the chair and sat down.

G. Change the *voice*:

1. The Tin Woodman stepped upon a beetle.

2. The Scarecrow oiled the Woodman's jaws.

3. He had been nearly crushed by the Lion's great jaws.

4. He became greatly frightened at this.

5. Oz will give the Tin Woodman a heart.

The Pobble Who Has No Toes

The Pobble who has no toes
Had once as many as we;
When they said, 'Someday you may lose them all,'
He replied — 'Fish fiddle de-dee!'
And his Aunt Jobiska made him drink
Lavender water *tinged* with pink,
For she said, 'The World in general knows
There's nothing so good for a Pobble's toes!'

The Pobble who has no toes,
Swam across the Bristol Channel;
But before he set out he wrapped his nose
In a piece of *scarlet flannel*.
For his Aunt Jobiska said, 'No harm
Can come to his toes if his nose is warm;
And it's perfectly known that a Pobble's toes
Are safe — provided he *minds* his nose.'

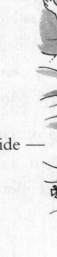

The Pobble swam fast and well,
And when boats or ships came near him,
He tinkledy-binkledy-winkled a bell,
So that all the world could hear him.
And all the Sailors and Admirals cried,
When they saw him nearing the further side —
'He has gone to fish for his Aunt Jobiska's
Runcible Cat with crimson *whiskers*!'

But before he touched the *shore*,
The shore of the Bristol Channel,

A sea-green Porpoise carried away

His *wrapper* of scarlet flannel.

And when he came to *observe* his feet,

Formerly *garnished* with toes so *neat*,

His face at once became *forlorn*

On perceiving that all his toes were gone!

(From The Pobble Who Has No Toes by Edward Lear)

A. Read the poem and answer the following questions:

1. What did the Pobble's Aunt Jobiska make him drink?
2. What did the Pobble do before he set out to swim across the Bristol Channel?
3. What keeps a Pobble's toes safe?
4. What did the Pobble do when boats and ships came near him?
5. What did the Sailors and Admirals think the Pobble had set out to do?
6. What happened to the Pobble's scarlet flannel?
7. Why did the Pobble look forlorn?

B. Write a short *paragraph* on how the Pobble lost his toes. Begin the *paragraph* like this:

'The Pobble set out to cross the Bristol Channel. Before he left, he …..'

C. Pick out the *main* and *subordinate clauses* from the following sentences. Mention of what *kind* each *subordinate clause* is.

1. The Pobble who has no toes had once as many as we.
2. When boats and ships came near the Pobble, he rang a bell.
3. The Pobble's face became forlorn when he saw his feet without any toes.

D. Fill in the blanks with *appropriate prepositions* taken from the poem:

1. The sky at sunset was tinged .... pink.
2. 'Walking in the morning is good .... your health,' said Ramen.
3. Many people have swum .... the English Channel.

E. Pick out the *verbs* and their *subjects* from the following sentences. In the case of a *transitive verb*, mention its *object/s*. In the case of a *verb of incomplete predication*, point out the *complement*.

1. His Aunt Jobiska made him drink lavender water tinged with pink.
2. A sea-green Porpoise carried away his wrapper of scarlet flannel.
3. His face at once became forlorn.

F. Match the *words* with the *meanings* they have in the poem:

1. lavender   (a) to see and notice
2. tinged   (b) soft, loosely woven woollen cloth
3. wrapper   (c) tidy
4. scarlet   (d) a pale, purple colour
5. shore   (e) sad, unhappy
6. flannel   (f) a piece of material for covering or protection
7. minds   (g) long, stiff hairs that grow near the mouth of a cat
8. neat   (h) a bright, red colour
9. forlorn   (i) slightly coloured
10. whiskers   (j) the land along the edge of the sea
11. observe   (k) decorated
12. garnished   (l) takes care of; is careful about

G. Change the *tenses* of the *verbs* in the following sentences as directed:

1. The Pobble swam fast and well. (Change to *past continuous.*)
2. The World in general knows there is nothing so good for a Pobble's toes. (Change to *simple past.*)
3. He has gone to fish for his Aunt Jobiska's Runcible Cat. (Change to *present continuous.*)

H. How many names of *colours* can you pick out from the four stanzas? Make a list.

I. Change the voice:

1. Aunt Jobiska made the Pobble a drink.
2. All the world could hear him.
3. A sea-green Porpoise carried away his wrapper of scarlet flannel.

Test 2

A. Say which of the *verbs* in *bold letters* are *transitive* and which *intransitive*. In the case of *transitive* verbs, point out the *objects*. In the case of verbs of *incomplete predication*, point out the *complements*.

1. Kishen **told** him <u>what took place last night</u>.
2. <u>In the morning</u>, Ramen **bought** some fish and vegetables.
3. What **are** you **doing** <u>this afternoon</u>, Jayant?
4. **Give** us something, <u>hot and sweet</u>, to drink, please.
5. We **found** him sitting <u>under a tree</u>.
6. **Keep** <u>what I have told you</u> a secret.
7. The mountains **look** beautiful <u>at sunset</u>.
8. The boys, <u>who had not done their homework</u>, had to stay back after school and **finish** it.
9. Arka **loves** listening to music <u>before going to bed</u>.
10. Kalyan **opened** the door and found the postman standing outside.

B. Say which of the *underlined* groups of words in the above sentences are *phrases* and which *clauses*. Mention of what *kind* each is.

C. Fill in the blanks with *appropriate prepositions*:

1. The dog jumped .... the gate and ran .... the postman.
2. 'Go .... bed at eight and sleep .... a hard bed,' advised the doctor.
3. The ball rolled .... the table and came .... a stop.
4. Some of the boys ran .... the field and jumped .... the pond for a swim.
5. Raja could not see anything .... the dark and bumped .... a tree.

D. Punctuate the following:

suman said I am going home tomorrow

shanti asked him why he was going home so soon

i dont want to stay here anymore muttered suman

raju told him stay for a few days longer we shall try to help you

no exclaimed suman I am fed up

E. Change the *mode of narration*:

1. 'This will teach me a lesson,' said he, 'to look where I step. For if I should kill another bug or beetle, I should surely cry again, and crying rusts my jaws, so that I cannot speak.'

2. Aunt Jobiska said, 'The world in general knows that there's nothing so good for a Pobble's toes!'

3. The sailors and the Admirals cried, 'He has gone to fish for his Aunt Jobiska's Runcible Cat with crimson whiskers!'

F. Change the *voice*:

1. In the evening they brought Mrs Harris to him in a cart.

2. The mongoose may bite the child.

3. He was carried down a roadside ditch by the summer flood.

4. Some man had stolen her bicycle.

5. The Pobble's bell could be heard by all the world.

G. In each of the following sentences, there is *at least one error*. Correct the errors and rewrite the sentences.

1. Heidi saw some sheeps on the mountainside. They were not her, but belonged to somebody else.

2. Gopal has borrowed a pen of my and refuses to return him.

3. Theirs house is very big but my is quite small.

4. 'Please put some sugars in my tea,' Sheetal told to Sharmila.

5. 'I cant fight the Giant. Him is very big and me am small,' said Tom.

6. 'Take yours medicine and go to bed,' Ma said John.

7. 'Me have a dog and it's tail is curly and white,' said Rinky.
8. John took him bat and went to play crickets.
9. 'When is you coming with yours sister to visit we?' asked Sharmila.
10. 'Come and see ourselves soon. We are looking forward to yours visit,'
    Niti told to Deepa.

Conjunctions

A *conjunction* is a word or group of words that can join separate words, groups of words, or sentences. A *conjunction*, therefore, helps us to make what we want to say shorter and more pointed.

(a) Gopal **and** Kishan went to school.
(b) This is a house which is old **but** magnificent.
(c) Too much food **and** lack of exercise made Shyam fat.

In (a), the conjunction *and* joins two words: <u>Gopal</u>, <u>Kishan</u>. In (b), the conjunction **but** joins two words: <u>old</u>, <u>magnificent</u>. In (c), the conjunction *and* joins two groups of words: <u>Too much food</u>, <u>lack of exercise</u>.

Note that sentence (a) can be split into two sentences:

   (i) Gopal went to school.   (ii) Kishan went to school.

Similarly, sentence (b) can be split into two sentences:

   (i) This is a house which is old.   (ii) This is a house which is magnificent.

Sentence (c), however, cannot be split into two sentences. We cannot say:

   (i) Too much food made Shyam fat.   (ii) Lack of exercise made Shyam fat.

The reason is that Shyam's fatness has been caused <u>jointly</u> by 'too much food' and 'lack of exercise'. If Shyam had exercised, 'too much food' would not probably have made him fat. Similarly, only 'lack of exercise' would not probably have made Shyam fat. The two reasons have worked together, and so, cannot be separated.

Similarly, a sentence like 'Sita **and** Gita are sisters' cannot be split into two separate sentences though *and* joins the two words: <u>Sita</u>, <u>Gita</u>. We cannot say:

(i) Sita is a sister.   (ii) Gita is a sister.

Sentences (a) and (b) show how a conjunction may join separate sentences into one sentence.

Some conjunctions are made up of more than one word:

(d) *Not only* was Hari famous, *but also* rich.

(e) Sita was *not only* intelligent, *but also* hardworking.

(f) You can go *either* today *or* the day after tomorrow.

(g) *Neither* Shyam *nor* his brother was at home.

(h) Ram *as well as* John came to the birthday party.

Given below is a list of words and phrases that are often used as *conjunctions*:
as, if, though, because, as soon as, scarcely ... when, hardly ... before, no sooner ... than, both ... and, before, in order that, since, for

Warning: Some of these words and phrases can also be used as prepositions and/or adverbs.

Remember that usually:

1. A conjunction only joins.
2. A preposition shows us the relationship between two words and takes an object.
3. An adverb qualifies a verb, an adjective or another adverb.

Join each set of sentences with the *conjunction* given within brackets:

1. This town is small. It is very crowded. *(but)*
2. Ram comes home from office. He rests. *(after)*
3. Sunil is a good swimmer. Sumit is a good swimmer. *(and)*
4. The sun rises. The clouds will disappear. *(when)*
5. He wants to rest. He is tired. *(because)*
6. Joy did not apologize. He had done something wrong. *(though)*
7. Govinda is thin. He has a lot of strength. *(but)*

8. Come. See everything for yourself. *(and)*

9. It is Saturday. The office is closed. *(since)*

10. Switch on the air conditioner. It is very hot. *(for)*

11. Go home immediately. Your mother is looking for you. *(because)*

12. You are late. You have to wait till the doctor is free. *(since)*

13. I shall go. I am ready. *(when)*

14. You must practise. You are perfect. *(till)*

15. Let me wash the dishes. You clean the table. *(while)*

16. John boarded the train. It started. *(no sooner ... than)*
    [Hint: ...... had John boarded ...... started.]

17. He is intelligent. His brother is intelligent. *(both ... and)*

18. It is winter. It is quite warm. *(though)*

19. Consider everything carefully. Then make up your mind. *(before)*

20. Susan heard the news of her friend's illness.
    She rushed to the hospital. *(as soon as)*

21. Swapan wanted to join a university.
    He wanted to become an engineer. *(in order that)*
    [Hint: ...... might become an engineer.]

22. One should not waste water. Water is precious. *(because)*

23. The snake looked poisonous. It was harmless. *(but)*

24. Jeff closed the door. The bell rang again. *(hardly ... before)*
    [Hint: ...... had Jeff closed ...... again.]

25. Please call a doctor. I am feeling rather ill. *(for)*

26. Everybody is here. Let us start the meeting. *(since)*

27. You must have determination. You will surely succeed. *(if)*

28. Dr Deb had just sat down to dinner.
    He received an emergency call from the hospital. *(scarcely ... when)*
    [Hint: ...... had Dr Deb sat ...... hospital.]

29. Brush your teeth. Then go to bed. *(before)*

30. Ram started eating. The food was getting cold. *(as)*

Participles and Gerunds

20

Present Participles

You have come across many examples of the **–ing** forms of verbs being used as adjectives *(Book 4, Chapter 5)*:

(a) The **dying** <u>man</u> was taken to the hospital.

(b) Do not wake a **sleeping** <u>dog</u>.

In (a), **dying** qualifies the noun 'man'.   (verb **die** + **–ing**)

In (b), **sleeping** qualifies the noun 'dog'.   (verb **sleep** + **–ing**)

Such adjectives formed from verbs with the help of the suffix **–ing** are usually called *present participles*.

However, we find that:

1. Many **–ing** adjectives are formed from <u>a prefix + a verb</u>, like:

    (a) **outstanding** success   (out + **stand**; = very good or important)

    (b) **ongoing** project   (on + **go**; = continuing)

    (c) **overbearing** manner   (over + **bear**; = trying to control others in an unpleasant way)

2. The meaning of an **–ing** adjective may be a little different from the usual meaning of the verb from which it has been formed, like:

    (a) **moving** story   (= affecting deeply)

    (b) **trying** situation   (= annoying; difficult)

    (c) **haunting** music   (= unforgettable)

3. Some **–ing** adjectives are used in colloquial English only to express disapproval, like:

    (a) **blooming** mistake   (b) **raving** lunatic   (c) **blithering** idiot

4. Some adjectives ending in **–ing** do not have any corresponding verbs:

    (a) **cunning** animal   (= selfishly clever or crafty)

(b) **balding** man   (= becoming bald)

(c) **appetizing** food   (= making one feel hungry or thirsty)

For reasons like these, some grammarians like to use the name '**–ing adjectives**' rather than '*present participles*' to refer to all adjectives formed from verbs and ending in **–ing**.

To avoid confusion, they also call <u>all adjectives, which end in **–ing**</u> and which are not related to any verbs or have not been formed directly from any verbs, '**–ing adjectives**'.

Warning: Remember that the **–ing** form of a verb is also used to form the continuous tenses. However, in such a case, a helping verb has to be used with the **–ing** form.

Past Participles

The *past participle* form of a verb may end in **–d**, **–ed**, **–en**, **–n**, or **–t** (*Book 4, Chapter 5*). This form of a verb may also be used as an **adjective**:

(a) The **wounded** <u>tiger</u> left a trail of blood.

(b) The **stolen** <u>goods</u> were recovered by the police.

(c) The **lost** <u>treasure</u> was discovered by Tom.

In (a), **wounded** qualifies the noun 'tiger'.

It is a *past participle*:   verb **wound** + **–ed**

In (b), **stolen** qualifies the noun 'goods'.

It is a *past participle*:   verb **steal** (past tense: **stole**) + **–n**

In (c), **lost** qualifies the noun 'treasure'.

It is a *past participle*:   verb **lose** + **–t**

The *past participle* forms of many verbs are the <u>same</u> as their *past tense* forms:

(d) The bullet only **wounded** the tiger and did not kill it.

(e) He **lost** all the money that his father had given him.

Secondly, the *past participle* form is also used with other helping verbs to form the **perfect tenses**:

(f) I **have lost** my book.   (*present perfect*: <u>have</u> + **lost**)

(g) The hunter **had** only **wounded** the tiger.   (*past perfect*: <u>had</u> + **wounded**)

So, to avoid confusion, when the *past participle* form of a verb is used as an **adjective**, some grammarians call it an '**–ed adjective**'. So, **–ed adjectives** include all adjectives formed from verbs and ending in **–d, –ed, –en, –n,** or **–t.**

As in the case of an **–ing** adjective, the meaning of an **–ed** adjective may be different from the usual meaning of the corresponding verb, or there may be no corresponding verb at all, like:

(a) **landed** property   (noun **land** + **–ed**; = related to land)

(b) **wooded** area   (noun **wood** + **–ed**; = covered with trees)

(c) **cold-blooded** killer   (= cruel, heartless)

(d) **warm-hearted** person   (= kind, friendly)

(e) **hooded** snake   (= having a hood)

(f) **hung** jury   (= unable to come to a decision; meaning different from the usual meaning of the verb 'hang')

(g) **beloved** leader   (no corresponding verb 'belove')

(h) **parched** land   (no corresponding verb 'parch')

The name **–ed adjective** is, therefore, also used to refer to <u>all adjectives</u> that end in **–d, –ed, –en, –n,** or **–t,** but which are not formed directly from any verb or which do not have any corresponding verb at all.

Remember that:

(i) If the **–d, –ed, –en, –n,** or **–t** form of a verb is used as an **adjective**, it is called a *past participle* or an **–ed** adjective.

(ii) The *past participle* form is used to form the **perfect tenses**.

(iii) The *past tense* form of a verb may be the same as the *past participle* form.

Warning: You must see how the *–d*, *–ed*, *–en*, *–n*, or *–t* form has been used. If it has been used <u>alone</u>, it is the **simple past tense** form of a verb.

If it has been used as an <u>adjective</u>, or with another <u>helping verb</u>, it is an *–ed* **adjective** or the *past participle* form of the verb concerned.

A. Pick out the *–ing* and *–ed* adjectives from the following sentences, and mention the *nouns* they qualify:

1. I remembered the forgotten song when Sita hummed the tune.
2. The experienced engineer has submitted a written report.
3. The cunning fox was trying to escape with the chicken it had stolen.
4. The injured man made a surprising statement.
5. The wounded soldier was lying on a broken bed.
6. Geeta bought a painted vase and put some fresh flowers in it.
7. Molten lava poured out of the erupting volcano.
8. Armed robbers raided the bank, broke open the locked deposit boxes and escaped with a lot of money.
9. The storm burst and the howling wind raged through the forest.
10. The escaped prisoner spent the night in a freshly dug ditch.
11. The frightened rabbit hid under a fallen tree.
12. The loaded gun went off, but nobody was hurt.
13. Jayant opened the closed door and saw a horrifying sight.
14. This book is full of amazing facts and amusing stories.
15. The badly spelt letter is obviously not written by an educated person.

Use of *–ing* and *–ed* Adjectives

An *–ing* adjective used in a phrase may have an **object**:

(a) What is the name of the boy <u>playing the violin</u>?
(b) The girl, <u>picking flowers</u>, is called Rita.
(c) The teacher, <u>teaching the pupils mathematics</u>, is quite well-known.

In (a), the phrase **playing the violin** qualifies the noun 'boy'.
The *–ing* adjective **playing** has an object: **violin**.
[Q: playing what/whom?   Ans: *violin*]

In (b), the phrase **picking flowers** qualifies the noun 'girl'.

The **–ing** adjective **picking** has an object: **flowers**.

[Q: picking what/whom?   Ans: *flowers*]

In (c), **teaching the pupils mathematics** qualifies the noun 'teacher'.

The **–ing** adjective **teaching** has two objects:

[Q: teaching what?   Ans: *mathematics* (direct object)

 Q: teaching whom?   Ans: *pupils* (indirect object)]

Such a group of words which contains an **–ing** or **–ed** adjective that makes the whole group act like an adjective is called an *adjective* or *participial phrase* (Phrases: Chapters 10 and 11).

Given below are examples of **adjective phrases** containing **–ed** adjectives (past participles):

(a) We staged a play <u>written by one of our friends</u>.

(b) In summer one should wear clothes <u>made of cotton</u>.

(c) The people rebuilt the town <u>destroyed by the enemy</u>.

In (a), **written by one of our friends** qualifies the noun 'play'. It contains the **–ed** adjective **written**.

In (b), **made of cotton** qualifies the noun 'clothes'. It contains the **–ed** adjective **made**.

In (c), **destroyed by the enemy** qualifies the noun 'town'. It contains the **–ed** adjective **destroyed**.

Use of the –*ing* form as a Noun: Gerund

The **–ing** form of a verb may also be used as a **noun**.

You know that only a noun, or a word or group of words acting like a noun can be the <u>subject</u> or <u>object</u> of a *verb*. Now, look at the following sentences:

(a) **Reading** <u>is</u> a good habit.

(b) I <u>like</u> **writing** essays.

In (a), **Reading** is the subject of the verb <u>is</u>. So, it is acting as a noun, and it is formed from the verb **read** + **–ing**.

In (b), **writing** is the object of the verb <u>like</u>. So, it is acting like a noun, and it is formed from the verb **write** + **–ing**.

When the **–ing** form of a **verb**, is used as a noun, it is known as a **gerund**. A gerund is also known as a **verbal noun**, for it can take an object like a verb:

(c) **Reading** <u>storybooks</u> is a good habit.

(d) I like **writing** <u>essays</u>.

In (c), <u>storybooks</u> is the object of **reading**.
[Q: reading *what*?   Ans: *storybooks*]
In (d), <u>essays</u> is the object of **writing**.
[Q: writing *what*?   Ans: *essays*]

B. Pick out the *gerunds* from the following sentences and point out their *objects*, if any:

1. Walking is good for health.
2. Ram does not like writing reports.
3. Talking is not allowed in the library.
4. Building a bridge requires knowledge and skill.
5. Sita loves singing sad songs.
6. He is fond of listening to music.
7. Planting trees and caring for them should be encouraged.
8. Playing football in this heat will make you ill.
9. I hate sleeping in the afternoon.
10. Our grandmother was very good at telling stories.

11. Driving long distances without rest is dangerous.
12. Acting in films and plays made him famous.
13. Mona Lisa is a famous painting by Leonardo da Vinci.
14. Cleaning the windows, sweeping the floors, and watering the plants were Mary's duties.

Faithful John

21

The young king was carrying home his bride – the daughter of the King of The Golden Palace. As the ship sailed, Faithful John sat on the *deck* playing his flute.

Suddenly three crows flew down and *perched* on a railing. Faithful John put down his flute and began to listen to the crows for he could understand the language of all animals.

'There is the king, carrying home his bride,' said the first crow. 'But he is not home yet.'

'What do you mean?' said the second crow.

'As soon as he steps ashore,' continued the first crow, 'a snow-white horse will come galloping up. The moment the king *mounts* it, the horse will fly away with the king and he will never be heard of again.'

'Can nothing *save* him?' asked the third crow.

'If some brave man throws himself in front of the horse and cuts off the head of the animal, the king will be saved. But if anyone tells the king this, he will be turned into stone from his toes to his *knees*,' the first crow said.

'But the king will still be in danger,' said the second crow. 'At the palace, he will be offered a beautiful golden shirt to wear. If the king wears it, he will be burnt to death.'

'How can he be saved?' asked the first crow.

'If some brave man picks up the shirt and *flings* it into the fire, the king will be saved,' said the second crow. 'But if anyone tells the king about this, he will be turned to stone from his knees to his heart.'

'I know more,' said the third crow. 'After the wedding, there will be a dance. At the dance, the young queen will fall *senseless*. Unless some brave man picks her up and takes three drops of blood from her throat and throws the blood away, she will die.'

'Will she live if someone takes the drops of blood?' asked the first crow.

'Yes,' replied the third crow. 'But if any man tells the king this, he will be turned to stone from the crown of his head to the tips of his toes.'

Faithful John heard all this in sorrow and made ready to give his life for his king.

(Adapted from *Grimms' Fairy Tales*)

A. Read the passage and answer the following questions:

1. What danger to the king did the first crow predict?
2. How could the king be saved from the horse?
3. What would happen to the person who told the king about the horse?
4. What would happen to the king if he wore the golden shirt? How could the king be saved?
5. What would happen to the person who told the king about the golden shirt?
6. What would happen at the dance? How could the queen be saved?
7. What would happen to the person who told the king how to save the queen?

B. Read the passage carefully once again. In three brief *paragraphs* complete the story and describe how Faithful John saved the king and queen. Your story must be written in the past tense. You may begin:

'Just as the crows had predicted, a snow-white horse came galloping up as soon as the king stepped ashore. The king was about to mount the horse when Faithful John ....'

C. Are the following statements *true* or *false*?

1. Faithful John sat on the deck and played a violin.
2. Four crows came and perched on the railing.
3. The first crow said that a snow-white horse would come galloping up to the king.
4. The second crow said that the king would be offered a golden shirt to wear at the palace.
5. The person who told the king about the golden shirt would be turned into a crow.
6. The third crow said that nothing could save the queen.
7. Faithful John decided to save the king.

D. Tick the correct *meaning* of each of the following *words* as used in the passage:

1. deck
   (a) any of the floors of a ship
   (b) a balcony
   (c) ten years

2. perch
   (a) a place to keep money
   (b) to sit or rest on something
   (c) a kind of fish

3. mount
   (a) to get on a horse
   (b) a mountain
   (c) to feel sorry

4. fling
   (a) to dance
   (b) a hard stone
   (c) to throw

5. senseless
   (a) fewer
   (b) unconscious
   (c) upset

6. knee
   (a) to bend down
   (b) something to open a lock with
   (c) the joint between the upper and lower parts of the leg

7. save   (a) to rescue

                (b) to collect

                (c) a sea wave

E. Change the following from *direct* to *indirect speech*:

1. 'What do you mean?' said the second crow.
2. The first crow said, 'A snow-white horse will come galloping up. The moment the king mounts it, the horse will fly away with the king and he will never be heard of again.'
3. 'Yes,' replied the third crow. 'But if any man tells the king this, he will be turned to stone from the crown of his head to the tips of his toes.'

F. Pick out the *verbs* from the following sentences and name their *tenses*:

1. The young king was carrying home his bride.
2. Suddenly three crows flew down and perched on the railing.
3. If some brave man picks up the shirt and flings it into the fire, the king will be saved.

G. Pick out the –ing adjectives from the following sentences and mention their *objects*, if any:

1. Faithful John, playing the flute, sat on the deck.
2. There is the king, carrying home his bride.

H. Identify the *voice*:

1. He will never be heard of again.
2. The king will be saved.
3. The horse carried the king away.
4. Faithful John was playing the flute.
5. The man will be burnt to death.

I. Change the *voice*:

1. He will never be heard of again.
2. The horse carried the king away.
3. Faithful John was playing the flute.

Whitewashing a Fence

Tom was given the *chore* of whitewashing thirty yards of *fence* on a sunny Saturday afternoon. And what was worse — it was one of those warm summer days when everyone else was out playing ball or swimming. And there was Tom, all alone on the sidewalk with a long-handled brush and a bucket of whitewash.

He looked at the fence. It seemed *enormous*, and he knew it would take all day to give it only one coat. Tom began to think of all the fun he had planned for the day, and he felt even more sorry for himself. Soon his friends would come down the street, and he *shuddered* to think of how they would laugh to see him whitewashing a fence on such a beautiful day. There had to be a way out of this situation!

Tom emptied his pockets and looked at his worldly wealth — bits of toys, marbles, and *trash*. He might be able to bribe someone else to help him for a while, but there wasn't nearly enough to buy a whole day of freedom. Tom thought for a while…then an *inspiration* burst upon him!

He picked up the brush and began to *spread* the whitewash slowly over the fence. In a few minutes, Ben Rogers came walking by, eating a big, juicy red apple. Tom's mouth watered at the sight of the fruit, but he kept on painting and pretended not to see or hear Ben at all.

'Hey there, Tom, what's up with you?' called Ben. 'It's too bad you have to work on a day like this. I'm just on my way to the river for a swim.'

Tom looked at Ben for a moment, then said, 'What do you call work?'

'Why, isn't that work?' asked Ben, pointing to the fence.

'Well maybe it is, and maybe it isn't,' answered Tom. 'All I know is that it suits me just fine.'

'Come on now, don't tell me you actually like it!'

'*Like* it? Well, I don't see why I shouldn't like it. It isn't every day that a boy gets to whitewash a fence.'

That put things in a new light for Ben. He stopped eating his apple and began watching Tom work. Maybe there was something to this whitewashing after all, he thought.

'Hey, Tom, let me try it for a while,' Ben asked.

'No, no!' protested Tom. 'Aunt Polly entrusted this fence to me, and I can't just let anyone take over such a big job.'

But Ben continued to beg Tom to let him have the *privilege* of whitewashing for just a little while. Tom kept refusing until Ben offered him the rest of his juicy red apple. That was what Tom had been waiting for.

Tom sat in the shade and *munched* the apple while Ben swished the brush back and forth, *sweating* at his work. As other boys came by, Tom kept trading with them, too, for a go at whitewashing the fence.

By mid-afternoon, the fence was completely whitewashed, and Tom was the proud owner of all sorts of treasures. His inspiration had certainly worked. All he had to do was make his chores seem to be fun, and the other boys were eager to do them for him.

(Adapted from *The Adventures of Tom Sawyer* by Mark Twain)

A. Read the passage and answer the following questions:

1. What work was Tom given to do? What made it worse?
2. What made Tom feel really sorry for himself and look for a way out of the situation?

3. Why did Tom empty his pockets?

4. How did Tom trick Ben into whitewashing the fence for him?

5. What did Tom take as a bribe from Ben?

6. What inspiration did Tom have? How did this inspiration make him the proud owner of all sorts of treasures?

B. Underline the *conjunctions* in the following sentences:

1. He stopped eating his apple and began watching Tom work.

2. He might be able to bribe someone else to help him for a while, but there wasn't nearly enough to buy a whole day of freedom.

C. Match each *word* with the *meaning* it has in the passage:

1.	chore	(a)	to eat steadily with much movement of the jaw
2.	fence	(b)	a special right or advantage
3.	enormous	(c)	perspiring
4.	shuddered	(d)	an unpleasant or boring task
5.	trash	(e)	to (use something to) cover a large area
6.	inspiration	(f)	shook (with horror or embarrassment)
7.	spread	(g)	rails or posts round a garden or field
8.	privilege	(h)	a sudden good idea
9.	munch	(i)	rubbish
10.	sweating	(j)	huge

D. Change the *tenses* of the underlined *verbs* as directed:

1. Tom <u>sat</u> in the shade and <u>munched</u> the apple. (Change to *future continuous*.)

2. He <u>looked</u> at the fence. (Change to *present perfect*.)

3. Tom <u>emptied</u> his pockets. (Change to *past perfect*.)

E. Rewrite the following, using the full forms of the *contractions*:

'Hey there, Tom, what's up with you?' called Ben. 'It's too bad you have to work on a day like this. I'm just on my way to the river for a swim.'

Tom looked at Ben for a moment, then said, 'What do you call work?'

'Why, isn't that work?' asked Ben pointing to the fence.

'Well maybe it is, and maybe it isn't,' answered Tom.

F. Change into *indirect speech*:

1. Tom answered, 'All I know is that it suits me just fine.'
2. 'Isn't that work?' asked Ben.
3. 'Tom, let me try it for a while,' Ben asked.

Writing a Letter

23

Writing a Letter

In Book 4 you have learnt how to write a simple personal letter. Let us go over what you have learnt about the **form** of a letter.

The information that is essential in a letter is the following:

1. The address from which you are writing the letter
2. The date on which you are writing the letter
3. The name of the person you are writing to or addressing
4. The address of the person to whom you are writing the letter
5. Your own name

These different items of information are placed in different places of the sheet of paper on which you are writing your letter. You will now be told of only one way in which this can be done.

Secondly, what other information you should give, where you should place it, and how you should arrange it depend on what kind of a letter you are writing and to whom. You will learn a variety of forms used in writing a letter as you go up to higher classes.

Note:

(a) Nowadays, the address is written without putting a comma after the number of your house: **37 South Road**

(b) In writing the date, the day comes first, followed by the month and the year. No comma is used between the month and the year: **11 August 2001**. If you use only numbers, then full stops are used: **11. 8. 2001**

1. Imagine you are in a boarding school and you want to write a letter to your father or mother, requesting him/her to send you some more pocket money. Your letter would probably read something like this:

Hill View School
Darjeeling
22 August 2001

Dear Papa,

You will be pleased to know that the results of my First Term Examinations are out and I have done quite well. You will, of course, receive the Report Card by post.

Papa, I need some more pocket money. My friend Rohan has a birthday coming up and I would like to give him the first book of the Harry Potter series – 'Harry Potter and the Philosopher's Stone'. I think the book costs around Rs 200.

Rohan is my special friend, and his parents always remember to send me a gift on my birthday and some extra tuck with him to share with me after the holidays.

I am sorry that I have spent almost all the pocket money that you gave to Matron for me at the start of the term. I have been treating myself and my friends at the School canteen. I promise to be more careful from now on and will buy whatever I need without asking for more. Matron has also scolded me for being so careless with money.

How are Mummy and Rinky? I do miss you all but school is a lot of fun, too.

Your loving son,
Arjun

You will note that your own address and the date have been written in the upper right-hand corner of the letter. You have ended your letter with **Your loving son**, the first letter of which – **Y** – is a capital letter. The rest of the words have been spelt with small letters. A comma comes after **son** and your own name is written underneath.

The letter should be addressed like this:

Mr J. Dasgupta
4/1 Baker Avenue
Kolkata 700 072

2. We are now going to learn how to write a letter that is not quite as informal as a letter to a friend, parent or close relative. Look at the following example:

37 South Road
Dehradun
11 August 2001

Dear Mr Sinha,

My little sister and I pass your house every day on our way to school. Every morning a large dog comes bounding out of your house and barks at us. Sometimes, it has even slipped out through the gate and come right up to us. Both of us are very scared of dogs and we would be very grateful if you could kindly keep your dog indoors, especially in the morning.

Thank you.

Yours sincerely,
Ramnath Srivastava

As in the other letters you have learnt to write, you give your own address and the date in the upper right-hand corner. You address the gentleman as **Mr Sinha**, because you do not know him, and he is an older person and should be shown respect. The **subscription** – that is, the part which comes at the end – in such letters is usually: **Yours sincerely**. Please note that the **Y** in **Yours** is a capital **Y**. The rest of the letters are small, as are the letters in **sincerely**. There is no apostrophe in the word: **Yours**. All formal letters that you write should carry your full signature, giving both your name and surname.

The letter should be addressed to:

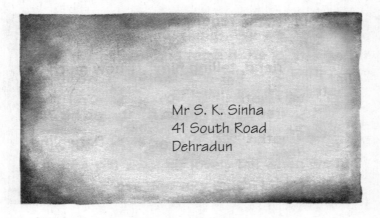

Mr S. K. Sinha
41 South Road
Dehradun

There is no need to paste a stamp on the envelope as you would have to do when you intend to send a letter by post. A note like this is usually put into an envelope and slipped into a letter box or delivered personally.

A letter which has been written politely usually gets a polite reply. Here is an example:

41 South Road
Dehradun
13 August 2001

Dear Ramnath,

I am so sorry that my Bingo has been bothering you. He is an Alsatian and a very gentle and playful dog. He is also a little naughty and manages to get out of the garden whenever some careless person leaves the gate open.

I would not like him to frighten you and your sister at all. I shall most certainly see to it that he is kept within the confines of my garden and that the gate is kept firmly locked so that he cannot get out. He must have been frightening other people as well and I should have been more careful.

May I make a suggestion? Why don't you and your sister come over to my house during the holidays and make friends with Bingo. This will help you to get over your fear of dogs and you will realize that he meant you no harm. My wife and I shall be very pleased to have you over.

With good wishes,

Yours sincerely,
Sunil Sinha

This note is addressed to:

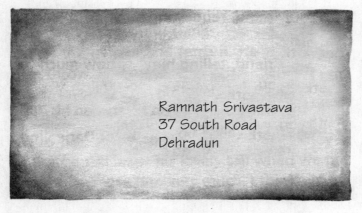

Ramnath Srivastava
37 South Road
Dehradun

Like the previous envelope, this also does not need a stamp.

Write a letter to:

1. Your Class Teacher apologizing for misbehaving in class
2. Your uncle about your efforts to help the victims of the *tsunami* disaster
3. A friend's mother requesting her to let your friend spend a week with you during the coming summer vacation
4. A neighbour requesting him to keep the volume of his television set low
5. A friend describing your new bicycle
6. A friend about a new hobby of yours
7. The captain of your school cricket team requesting him to let you play for your school

Writing an Autobiography

24

It is easy to tell other people something about yourself. But suppose you were told to imagine that you were somebody else — another person, or even perhaps, an animal or a thing, and asked to tell the story of your life. What would it be like? Perhaps, something like this:

The Autobiography of a School Desk

I have just been placed in a gloomy, dark room. They call it an attic. In the dim light I can see some of my old friends. There is old Scar-top in the corner and there is poor Sal. She was so beautiful once upon a time. But then, I also was a handsome, brown desk once.

Years ago – such a long, long time ago – I was part of a sturdy oak tree. Some nasty men came and cut it down. They sawed off the part of the tree which had me in it and carried it to a place they called a factory. Oh! How they hurt me there! They cut out flat portions of me. Then they left me to dry and they planed me out and then nailed bits of me together. I now had a flat top and four strong legs. They called me a desk. Then they polished me a dark brown colour. I rather liked the smell of varnish, and when they finished, I looked quite handsome. I stood in a line with a lot of my brothers and sisters ready to be taken away.

I was bought by a school called 'Green Valley'. I was placed in the front row of a room they called Class 5. It was a pleasant, airy room and I stood by a window with pretty, checked curtains. A bench, also made of wood, was put behind me. One of the smart desks told me that her name was Sal. She was really pretty. All boys and girls think that we are all the same, but we are not. We are as different from each other as you are. An old desk behind me looked awful – it had a horribly scarred surface. He was known as old Scar-top and he was one of the senior desks. He warned us not to be too proud of our appearance as we would soon look like him. We did not believe him then.

One morning a group of happy, laughing children came into the room. Two of them put their books on me. 'Bags, this place is ours!' one of them cried to the other. They were good friends. I wish I could tell you about all that they said, the secrets they shared and the notes they passed under me to each other when class was going on. They treated me very well and I remember my first pupils with love. There were many others who cared for me, too, and I wish I could tell you about them all.

But then came the naughty ones! Year after year they hurt me dreadfully by scratching me with pencils and sharp dividers. One night, after school, I was groaning in pain when old Scar-top said, 'Don't worry. The pain will go away but the marks will not. Look at me.'

One terrible morning, a group of naughty pupils climbed on top of Sal and began to jump! There was a sickening, cracking sound and one of Sal's delicate legs collapsed under her. The boys ran away. The next day Sal was taken away. She came back after her leg was mended but she was never as beautiful as she once had been.

Year after year, I stood in the class. I am so proud of the students who worked on me and did so well at school like Sohail, Sharon, Saurav, Eesha and Ruby. There were so many more. I have heard that Saurav is a doctor, now. I wish I could show him some of my aching joints!

Then one day, we heard whispers that the school was going to be smartened up. They were going to get new desks and benches made of 'fibre glass' or 'plastic' or something like that. Even our old companion the blackboard was to go and a new board was to come. Soon after these rumours, some workmen came into the room. We knew what was going to happen and looked around the room one last time, remembering the laughter and the tears, the noise and the bustle, and the wonderful feeling that we were helping to teach children to be good and strong men and women of the future. We were taken to the attic I have told you about before.

We lie here not really knowing what is going to happen to us now. Some say that we shall be sold or given away to another school. Scar-top says that we shall all end up being burnt for fuel. I hope not. I would not mind going to another school to make a new start with new pupils. But who knows what will happen to me!

What you have just read is called an **autobiography**. The word **autobiography** is made up of **auto + bio + graphy**:

auto— is a Greek prefix and one of its meanings is *(something) produced by oneself or self-produced*.

bio— comes from a Greek word, one of the meanings of which is *life*.

—graphy is a Greek suffix, one of the meanings of which is *writing*.

So, an **autobiography** is the story or an account of a person's life written by that person himself/herself.

If you write the story of Mahatma Gandhi's life, it will be a **biography**. *The Story of My Experiments with Truth*, which is an account of Mahatma Gandhi's life written by Gandhiji himself, is an **autobiography**. In a higher class you will learn how to write biographies.

When you are asked to write an autobiography, what you are being really asked to do is to imagine that you are that person or thing, and you are telling the story of the life of that person or thing to somebody else.

There are one or two things you must remember when writing autobiographies:

1. The title must be simple and clear:

   The Autobiography of a Pet Cat   or

   The Autobiography of a Blackboard

   You must spell out clearly that this is not an ordinary composition but an autobiography. Write the title in capital letters. This is the easiest form.

There are other ways of writing a title which you will learn later on.

2. You must use the same method that you use in writing a composition: think about what you are going to write and then jot down your thoughts in the form of points in your rough book, or if your teacher permits, in your fair exercise book. You can then arrange your autobiography into:
(a) **introduction**, (b) **body** (in more than one paragraph if you wish) and (c) **conclusion**.

3. Remember to divide your composition into paragraphs – each paragraph should deal with one particular point. For example, paragraphs 2 and 3 of **The Autobiography of A Desk** would come under the headings:
(i) **How I became a desk** and (ii) **Introduction to my mates in a new classroom**.

Once you have learnt how to note down your thoughts and organize them quickly, you will find that writing a composition is not as difficult as you think it to be! You will soon be able to divide your composition into paragraphs quite easily and the discipline will help you to express yourself better when you answer questions on other subjects like History, Geography, Literature, etc.

A. Write an *autobiography* of each of the following:

1. A Pencil
2. A Blackboard
3. A School Bag
4. A Pair of Shoes
5. A Tree
6. A Pet Dog
7. An Old Palace
8. A Circus Clown
9. A Boat

B. Write an *essay* on each of the following topics:

1. A Bad Dream
2. A Walk Through the Rain
3. A Thunderstorm
4. Newspapers
5. A Journey in a Crowded Bus
6. On Reading Storybooks
7. A Person I Respect
8. Music That I Enjoy
9. My Ambition
10. Brothers and Sisters

Writing a Story and a Dialogue

25

Writing a Story

Usually when you are asked to write a story, you are given an outline. There are a few simple rules that you need to follow when writing a story:

1. Your story must have a title.
2. You should write your story in the *past tense* as you are narrating an event that has already taken place.
3. Introduce characters, unless they are already given to you in the outline, and give them names. This will make your story more interesting.
4. Introduce some conversation in **direct speech**.
5. You may use **contractions** and **interjections** in conversation.
6. You should be very clear about the plot for it must be developed in a coherent manner. Otherwise, you may ramble and confuse yourself.
7. The words you use should be carefully chosen to help create an appropriate atmosphere or heighten the effect you are aiming at.

A story may be developed from a given **introduction**. For example:
A flash of lightning lit up the dark sky. Looking up, they saw ....

Quite naturally, you are not expected to describe a cricket match on a sunny morning! You must follow the given line.

Alternatively, you may be given a **title** like: **An Unwelcome Visitor**
The story that you choose to write must suit the title.

A. Develop each *outline* into a story:

1. Rich old lady becomes blind – calls doctor – doctor asks for huge fee – lady agrees to pay if cured – doctor comes daily – admires lady's furniture – removes a piece every day – lady finally cured – refuses to pay doctor –

doctor goes to court – lady tells judge she is not fully cured – cannot see furniture – judge realizes what has happened – doctor punished

2. Young English soldier taken captive by the French – allowed to wander alone on beach – homesick and misses mother – makes little boat out of wooden cask – caught by guards – taken to Napoleon – Napoleon impressed by boy's love for mother – ready to cross sea in frail boat – frees boy – gives him gold coin – boy treasures coin all his life

3. Soldier returns home – prisoner of war for many years – wanders about streets – heart full of love for his country – sees bird-seller in marketplace – variety of birds in cages – buys all the birds – sets them free – knows the value of freedom

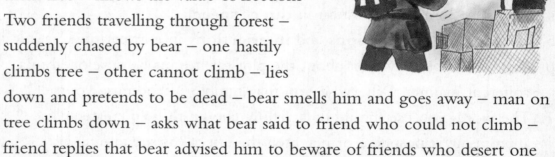

4. Two friends travelling through forest – suddenly chased by bear – one hastily climbs tree – other cannot climb – lies down and pretends to be dead – bear smells him and goes away – man on tree climbs down – asks what bear said to friend who could not climb – friend replies that bear advised him to beware of friends who desert one in time of need

5. Farmer on death-bed – sons always quarrel – man sends sons out to bring bundle of sticks – tells each to break the bundle – none can – tells each to break one – sons do so easily – tells them that united they will be strong – alone, each will break like a single stick – sons are ashamed

B. The *first line* of a story is given to you. Complete it and give it a *title*.

1. All the girls laughed.
2. The doorbell rang loudly.
3. The car screeched to a halt.
4. 'Don't believe him,' cried the boys.
5. 'I shall not go,' said Rahul, stubbornly.

C. Use each *title* to write a story:

1. Mischief
2. Rahul's Big Adventure
3. The Haunted House
4. The Mystery of the Missing Bag
5. My Aunt Bella

Writing a Dialogue

A dialogue is a conversation between two people. Sometimes you may be asked to write a dialogue between two animals or two inanimate objects. Keep in mind that there is always a difference between the spoken and written forms of language. When we speak, we use an easier and more colloquial form than we do when writing any formal composition.

Some of the rules that you must follow when writing a dialogue are:

1. Your language must be simple and direct, for a dialogue represents actual speech: two persons are speaking to each other as if in real life. Though your language may be racy and colloquial, avoid the use of slang.

2. You may use **contractions** and **interjections.**

3. When writing a dialogue, remember the situation in which you have to place it. Keep to the point and do not make your dialogue too long or involved.

4. Human characters must be given names. Use a colon (:) after the name of the speaker and then write the words spoken. (See example below.)

5. Since there are two characters, make sure that each gets a fair share of words to speak. The conversation should not be monopolized by any one character.

D. First read the following example of a *dialogue*. Then, write a *dialogue* between two friends who are planning a class party to be held on the last day of a school term.

Nisha : Sania, have you decided on the food?

Sania : Yes, but let's plan the decorations first.

Nisha : I've told Ajay, Tony and Vinita to bring balloons. Some of the others are bringing streamers and other things.

Sania : That's okay then, but we'd better be careful. We're not supposed to stick anything onto the walls. Tell Prema and Vijay to get lots of string. We'll just tie the streamers to the windows. Anyway, we'll need string for the balloons.

Nisha : We'll buy chips and Cheetos.

Sania : Oh! Please, please get some Kurkure. I simply love Kurkure.

Nisha : Sunita is bringing idli for everyone. Her mother makes delicious idlis.

Sania : Some of the others are bringing cheese and vegetable sandwiches.

Nisha : Yummy! What about sweets?

Sania : We'll have plenty of money left over to buy pastries and cold drinks.

Nisha : Oooh! My mouth is watering already. Just don't forget to tell Ashita and Shreya to get large packets. We have to collect everything after the party and put the packets in the dustbin. We shouldn't leave the class in a mess.

Sania : Don't worry. They'll get the packets. They're also getting the paper plates and cups.

Nisha : I can't wait till Wednesday! It's going to be a super party!

Write the following *dialogues*:

1. Between two friends about a television programme they both enjoy watching

2. Between two friends about a new classmate

3. A funny conversation between a horse and a cow

4. Between a cricket bat and a tennis racquet
   [You may give them names: *Bat* and *Racquet*.]

5. Between two friends about a gift that they are going to buy for a common friend on his/her birthday

6. A pupil has not done his homework. His teacher is annoyed. Write a dialogue between the pupil and the teacher.

7. Between two friends preparing for their annual examination

Writing a Diary

26

There are different kinds of diaries: they are used to remind one of appointments; they are used like planners in which people make entries about things to be done; they are used to record daily or monthly expenses. In your school diary you note down your homework, class assignments and days on which you have been absent from school.

A diary is also a personal record of events of your life, your thoughts and feelings. Some diaries have become famous literary works. *The Diary of Anne Frank* was written by a thirteen-year-old girl, Anne. The entries span two years during which Anne, her parents and sister, had to hide in a warehouse in Amsterdam in 1942. Anne died young but her diary was found and handed to Otto Frank, her father. The diary gives us a very human and touching account of people compelled to live in dreadful conditions in terrible times. *The Diary of Samuel Pepys*, later published in 11 volumes, gives a vivid picture of the life and times of the great English diarist who was born in 1633 and died in 1703.

In Book 4 you have been taught to address your diary as a friend, **Dear Diary.** Anne addressed her diary as **Dear Kitty**.

The Princess Diaries by Meg Cabot, *Desiree* by Ann Marie Selinko, and *The Diary of a Nobody* by George and Weedon Grossmith are some works of fiction written in the form of diaries.

Given below are three extracts.

A.

(Adapted from *The Diary of Anne Frank*)

Tuesday, 27 April 1943

The house is still trembling from the after-effects of the quarrels. Everyone is angry with everyone else. Mother and I, Mr. van Daan and Father, Mother and Mrs. van Daan. Terrific atmosphere, don't you think? ....

Our food is terrible. Breakfast consists of plain unbuttered bread and ersatz coffee. For the last two weeks, lunch has been either spinach or cooked lettuce with huge potatoes that have a rotten sweetish taste. If you are trying to slim, this is the place to be!

B.

(Adapted from *The Diary of a Nobody*)

April 27

Painted the bath red, and was delighted with the result. Sorry to say Carrie was not. She said she had never heard of such a thing as a bath being painted red......

April 29 Sunday

Woke up with a fearful headache and strong symptoms of a cold. I had got a chill, and decided to have a bath as hot as I could bear it. Bath ready – could scarcely bear it so hot. I got in; very hot but very acceptable. I lay still for some time. On moving my hand out of the water I experienced the greatest fright! Imagine my horror on discovering my hand full of blood! My first thought was that I was bleeding to death. My second thought was to ring the bell, but there was no bell to ring. My third thought was that it was nothing but the red enamel paint that had dissolved with the boiling water. I stepped out of the bath perfectly red all over. Must tell Farmerson to come on Monday and paint the bath white.

Make the following *entries* (a page each) in a diary:

1. On a street accident that you witnessed on your way to school
2. On a role you have to play in a drama to be staged in your school
3. On a book that you have just finished reading and liked very much
4. On your feelings the evening before you are to get your school Report Card
5. On a quarrel over a small and unimportant thing at home
   [How did the quarrel end? Was everything sorted out?]
6. On your feelings after an argument with your mother about what you should be given as tiffin in your school lunch box. You obviously do not like what is usually given to you, but your mother has a different opinion on the matter.
7. On the new Games Teacher of your school

E-Mail

27

A letter which is sent by post needs to have an envelope with the address of the receiver (*addressee*) on it. You also need to give the date and your own address in the letter, and follow a certain format.

Now we shall deal with a modern form of communication – the **e-mail**.

The body of your communication remains the same as in a letter whether you write to friends or relatives or whether the mail is more formal in nature. Let us look at the differences:

1. You do not need an envelope. You type a mail address such as 'zo_kha@hotmail.com' or a similar address. The address should be typed in the space marked: **TO**
2. Your own address, the date and time when the mail is sent are given automatically by the computer and need not be written separately.
3. What your e-mail is about should be written in the space marked: **SUBJECT**

Your computer teacher will teach you how to log on to a site.

When you communicate with a friend or relative, do the person the courtesy of doing so properly. Your mail should be clearly thought out, properly arranged in paragraphs, and typed neatly. Do not send a mail which reads: 'Wtng 4 U on wkend' or 'CEng U ws Gr8'. A mail like this has to be deciphered like a strange code. It also shows that you do not care enough about the person to spare him or her the time or patience to send a proper and clearly spelt-out mail. Always read what you have written before clicking the button **SEND**. A well-written mail can be stored in the form of a printout. It is as valuable as a letter or an entry in a diary.

While surfing the net, you may come upon sites that interest you. You may wish to become the member of a nature club, find other coin collectors, look for information on an African Safari for a school project, or just want to subscribe to a magazine about pets.

Look at the following example:

Send an e-mail to the given address enquiring about available coins:

shweta@coins_coins.com

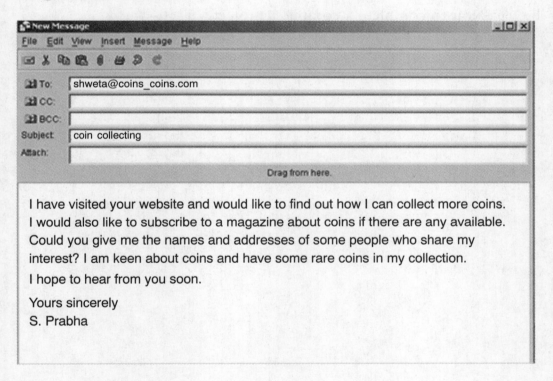

Send the following e-mails:

1. To your grandmother after you have returned from a holiday in the hills
2. To a friend about a new Computer Club in your school. Describe some of the activities of the club.
3. To a friend about a new shopping mall that has come up in your locality

4. To <u>dogmag!!@dogmagi.com</u> requesting them to enrol you as a subscriber to the magazine *PuppiesGuides.Com*. Give your postal address so that they can send you the magazine.

5. To <u>env.poll@naturecamp.net</u>, applying for enrolment in a two-week Nature Camp on environmental studies

6. To <u>visitusplz@asafari.net</u> for the names of some internet magazines on African wildlife, so that you may collect material for a school project

7. To an uncle, who is a computer engineer, thanking him for the help that he gave you to complete a computer project

Test 3

A. Give the –ing and *past participle* forms of the following *verbs*:

sing, hunt, give, read, agree, draw, eat, bend, burn, know, tell, tear, shut, sell, choose, steal, want, forget, escape, write

B. Fill in each blank correctly with an –ing or –ed adjective/noun formed from the *verb* given within brackets at the end of each sentence:

1. The mountains and the blue sky looked as beautiful as a .... picture. *(paint)*

2. We saw a little girl .... all alone in the rain. *(stand)*

3. Nilesh always looks happy and has a .... face. *(smile)*

4. The sun set and in the .... light we could hardly see where we were going. *(fade)*

5. A .... notice was given to each student. *(print)*

6. Shyam took the .... flowers out of the vase and threw them away. *(wither)*

7. Fill in the blanks in the sentences .... *(give)*

8. The man, ... vegetables, is honest in his dealings. *(sell)*

9. The team, ... for the big match, must practise every day. *(choose)*

10. We helped Ma by .... the dishes after the meal was over. *(wash)*

C. Fill in the blanks with suitable *adjectives* or *adverbs*:

1. .... do you think it will stop raining?

2. Come ...., for everybody is waiting for you.

3. '..................... book should I read to improve my English?' asked Kunal.

4. The play was .... boring and I fell asleep.

5. .... many know this secret?

6. .... house belongs to Vinod's uncle.

7. We have never heard .... a story before.

8. Put the book back .... you took it from.
9. '..................... Lord! I have left my bag in the taxi,' exclaimed Mahua.
10. The nurse told the doctor, '..................... patients are waiting for you.'

D. Change the *mode of narration*:

1. 'Who is sleeping in my bed?' asked Baby Bear.
2. Arjun said, 'Sorry! I have broken your pen.'
3. The manager told the watchmen, 'You must be alert and watchful.'
4. Rinky inquired, 'When shall I come this afternoon?'
5. Kushal replied, 'Please come tomorrow.'
6. Hari said, 'Ah! How peaceful this place is.'
7. Veena asked Swati whether she would like a cup of tea.
8. Rinky told Chandni to keep quiet.
9. The child asked his mother why the sky looks blue.
10. Jayant said that he would go to Delhi sometime that week.

E. Fill in the blanks with *appropriate prepositions*:

1. Trembling .... fright, Nishad hid .... the door.
2. 'Are you afraid .... ghosts? I laugh .... them,' boasted Arka.
3. 'The blue sky was .... us and the blue sea below, ' said the sailor.
4. 'Come, sit down .... the table and eat your dinner,' said Ma, smiling .... us.
5. Niti looked out .... the window and saw her father waiting .... a bus.
6. He was looking .... his lost suitcase all through the night.
7. The nurse looked .... the patient with great care.
8. This train never arrives .... time.
9. You are just .... time to see the champion receiving his prize.
10. If you look .... this telescope, you can see the rings .... Saturn,' said the astronomer.

F. Join each of the following sets of sentences by using the *conjunction* given within brackets at the end of the set:

1. It started raining. The match was abandoned. *(when)*

2. Roop cannot go to school. He is ill. (*because*)

3. Sanjay ran as fast as he could. He could not catch the bus. (*but*)

4. The boys want to play cricket. The boys want to play football. (*or*)

5. Sita poured the tea. Rita passed the sandwiches around. (*while*)

6. Everybody loved the great leader. They also respected him.
   (*not only … but also*)

7. Sita can stay with us. She can put up at a hotel. (*either … or*)

8. This meeting is a very important one. You must not miss it. (*since*)

9. The bookshop had just opened. Everybody rushed in to buy a copy of the
   book. (*no sooner … than*)

G. Fill in the blanks with *verbs* as directed. Remember that a *verb* must agree with its *subject* in *number* and *person*.

1. Where there .... a will, there .... a way. (simple present of *be*)

2. It .... to rain tonight. (present continuous of *go*)

3. At Delhi, we .... at a hotel. (future continuous of *stay*)

4. Anuj's father .... him a bicycle on his birthday. (simple past of *buy*)

5. Shyam .... when I arrived. (past continuous of *sleep*)

6. Geeta .... all her pocket money on books. (present perfect of *spend*)

7. Virendra .... dinner for us all. (future continuous of *cook*)

8. Varun .... to return the book to the library. (past perfect of *forget*)

9. If you start reading the book now, you .... it by tomorrow.
   (future perfect of *finish*)

10. They .... the villagers to build a hospital. (future continuous of *help*)

H. Fill in the blanks with appropriate forms of the *verbs* given within brackets:

1. .... tomorrow and I .... you how to solve the problem.
   (*come, show*)

2. Gopal .... to Mohan that he .... not come to school the
   next day. (*say, will*)

3. Where .... you .... such a beautiful clock? *(find)*

4. When the bell rang, Arjun .... still .... *(write)*

5. Ruchira .... the door when Chandni knocked. *(open)*

6. I am sure the mechanic .... the car by tomorrow. *(repair)*

7. '..................... not of tomorrow, ... of today,' said Mihir. *(think)*

8. Nobody .... much attention to somebody who .... too much. *(pay, talk)*

9. The train .... late and we have to wait until it arrives. *(run)*

10. Raktim .... a letter to his mother tomorrow. *(write)*

I. Say which underlined groups of words are *phrases* and which *clauses*. Also mention of what *kind* each is.

1. <u>Sitting in the examination hall</u>, Ram forgot everything <u>that he had read</u>.

2. 'The present, <u>which Rita has given me</u>, is wonderful!' said Niti.

3. Shiva was in great pain and could speak only <u>with great difficulty</u>.

4. Take the books <u>that you have brought</u> and go home.

5. That boy, <u>wearing a white shirt and black trousers</u>, is the one <u>who comes first in our class</u>.

6. The man <u>who speaks the truth</u> has nothing to fear.

7. <u>Screaming with delight</u>, the children ran towards the man <u>serving ice cream</u>.

J. There is at least one *error* in each of the following sentences. Correct the errors and rewrite the sentences.

1. The sun is rising in the east and setting in the west.

2. Deena has bought a lot of furnitures for her new flat.

3. John said Jeff the school is closed.

4. I think this book is more better than that.

5. Swapan inquired whether I had seen his brother tomorrow.

6 His friends told to him that they are going on a picnic.

7. 'Please help ourselves,' pleaded the refugees.